SUREŚVARA'S VĀRTIKA ON
ŚIŚU AND MŪRTĀMŪRTA BRĀHMAṆA

ADVAITA TRADITION SERIES

VOL. 7

Sureśvara's Vārtika on Śiśu and Mūrtāmūrta Brāhmaṇa

Edited, Translated and Annotated by
K.P. JOG
SHOUN HINO

MOTILAL BANARSIDASS PUBLISHERS
PRIVATE LIMITED • DELHI

First Edition: Delhi, 1996

ISBN: 81-208-1382-0

Also available at:

MOTILAL BANARSIDASS

41 U.A., Bungalow Road, Jawahar Nagar, Delhi 110 007
120 Royapettah High Road, Mylapore, Madras 600 004
16 St. Mark's Road, Bangalore 560 001
8 Camac Street, Calcutta 700 017
Ashok Rajpath, Patna 800 004
Chowk, Varanasi 221 001

PRINTED IN INDIA

BY JAINENDRA PRAKASH JAIN AT SHRI JAINENDRA PRESS,
A-45 NARAINA, PHASE I, NEW DELHI 110 028
AND PUBLISHED BY NARENDRA PRAKASH JAIN FOR
MOTILAL BANARSIDASS PUBLISHERS PRIVATE LIMITED,
BUNGALOW ROAD, DELHI 110 007

To

Shriman Koun Hino and Shrimati Kyoko Hino

With Love and Respect

श्रीमुखम्

भवन्तः भवदीयबृहदारण्यकोपनिषद्भाष्यवार्तिकांग्लानुवादैकदेशं श्री-जगद्गुरुचरणानां सन्निधौ समार्पयन् ।

शुक्लयजुश्शाखीयायां बृहदारण्यकोपनिषदि आत्मतत्त्वप्रतिपादनं वि-स्तृततया विहितं वर्तते । ब्रह्मविदामग्रणीः याज्ञवल्क्यैः विशिष्टया रीत्या अस्यामुपनिषदि तत्त्वं बोधयन् समुपलभ्यते । त्रय्यन्तसिद्धान्त प्रचारण-चणाः श्रीमच्छंकरभगवत्पादाचार्याः अस्या उपनिषदः अनवद्यं भाष्य-मरीरचन् । तेषां अन्तेवासिषु विद्यया वयसा च ज्येष्ठाः श्रीसुरेश्वरा चार्याः तस्य भाष्यस्य हृद्यं वार्तिकं व्यलिखन् । वार्तिकस्यास्य सम्यक्-परिशीलनेन वेदान्तसिद्धान्तः असन्देहं अवगन्तुं पार्यत इति निश्चप्रचं समेषाम् । अत एव अस्य वार्तिकस्य भावं लोकान् अवबुबोधयिषन्तो भवन्तःआंग्लानुवादं व्यधासिषुः ।

भवदीयोयमुद्यमःप्रशंसनीयो वर्तते । ग्रन्थोयं अपरिचितसुरगिरामपि लोकानां वार्तिकतात्पर्यावबोधनक्षमो भवतु, भवन्तश्च श्रेयःपरम्पराभिः-समेधन्तां ।

Private Secretary
To His Holiness Sri
Jagadguru Shankaracharya
of Shringeri

FOREWORD

The *Bṛhadāraṇyaka* is the biggest and most important one among principal Upaniṣads and contains numerous discussions of teachers, pupils, questioners and others. It is marked by philosophical speculations not opposed to but in conformity with a vigorous performance of rituals. The *Bṛhadāraṇyaka* reveals to us the towering personality of the great Upaniṣadic thinker Yājñavalkya who affirmed *neti neti*, i.e. indescribability of the Brahman, the ultimate Truth. It is on this basis that Śaṅkara built up his theory of Non-dualistic Vedānta.

Consequently, the Bhāṣya of Śaṅkara on this Upaniṣad has assumed a very great significance in Vedāntic literature. Next to his Bhāṣya on the *Brahmasūtra*– nay almost on a par with it–his Bhāṣya on this Upaniṣad is a vivid picture of the (almost aggressively) vigorous philosophical acumen of the great philosopher. And this is more pronouncingly felt in his references to and the refutations of the arguments of the followers of other systems of Indian philosophy, for they were unavoidable for him while he clarified (in his way—on the non-dualistic way) the thought of the Upaniṣad from which he was distant at least by a period of about 1000 years and since there had intervened between him and the Upaniṣad a number of thinkers of various systems. Yet, since he had set himself to the task of commenting on the Upaniṣad, he inevitably became somewhat brief, leaving quite a lot of disputations unclear (for his contemporaries).

This gave his pupil Sureśvara a scope for clarifying his Guru's thought in its fullness and he wrote the *Bṛhadāraṇyakopaniṣad-bhāṣyavārtika*. The last member of the compound-name, *vārtika*, refers to Sureśvara's discussion of *ukta*, *anukta* and *durukta* portions in Śaṅkara's writing. Sureśvara has underlined every small detail in the varied arguments in the Bhāṣya on the Upaniṣad and clarified the same with characteristic skill. It is noticed that Sureśvara is familiar with minute details of different philosophical systems—Nyāya and Mīmāṃsā, in particular—and therefore he has in a way shaped the Ṭīkā of Ānandagiri, the most read commentator of Śaṅkara's works, thus throwing abundant light on the vigorous philosophical activity of the times which preceded his teacher Śaṅkara and himself.

A special mention has to be made here of Sureśvara's detailed discussions of the views of Bhartṛprapañca, a predecessor or a senior contemporary of Śaṅkara. It may become possible for us, now, to set up a somewhat understandable scheme of Bhartṛprapañca's philosophy on the basis of these. Another significant contribution of Sureśvara deserves special notice. His discussions about the interpretation of Vedāntic passage (implying Mīmāṃsā) and various means of understanding/knowledge (implying Pramāṇavyavahāra or Nyāya) in relation to the Vedāntic logic indeed deserve in-depth studies for purposes of clarifying the method of Non-dualistic Vedānta.

The Vārtika of Sureśvara on the *Bṛhadāraṇyakopaniṣad* is truly his *magnum opus* and needed to be translated in full. I feel happy that Prof. K. P. Jog and his worthy pupil Dr. Shoun Hino have undertaken this important task. I have gone through the earlier parts of this work and find that they have well attempted to secure a satisfactory translation. This translation, I cannot forget to add, is accompanied by some brief annotation on the same. For this work Dr. Hino was awarded the 1991 Eastern Study Prize by the Eastern Institute, Inc. at the Indian Embassy in Tokyo.

Hajime Nakamura

PREFACE

Our translation of Śiśu and Mūrtāmūrta Brāhmaṇa 2.2 and 2.3 in BUBV goes to the press somewhat late and before Ajātaśatru Brāhmaṇa; this is owing to the sudden and quite a prolonged illness of K. P. Jog. Consequently, our introduction to BUBV 2.2 and 3, which depends much on the earlier Brāhmaṇa, viz. Ajātaśatru Brāhmaṇa is bound to be (in some measure) deficient. It takes for granted what is (or, will be) said in the introduction to that Brāhmaṇa; it relates more to the textual details than to the problems involved. That is to say, it is not clarified herein how BU (or, BUBV) 2.2 and 3 do not present any significantly positive philosophical thoughts in addition to those in BU (or, BUBV) 2.1; they merely amplify, by adding explanatory details, the thought in the latter.

A few words about our translation may not be unnecessary. There is inherent difficulty in rendering into very simple English structure the slightly (and comparatively) truncated or complex Sanskrit structure; we have yet tried at a number of places to simplify the same by avoiding as much literal English rendering as in the earlier parts of our series.

As usual our friends and colleagues in the Deccan College, Pune have helped us in tracing some citations. We acknowledge gratefully their help. We express our special thanks also to Prof. K. Macida (ILCAA), Prof. J. Takashima (ILCAA) and Mr. N. Okaguchi. Prof. Macida is a developer of Devanāgarī printing software called CATUR, which has been used in preparing our books, and Mr. Okaguchi is a Devanāgarī font designer.

We hope to put into our readers' hands the work on BUBV 2.1 at some early date.

Pune
Caitra Śuddha 2, Śake 1917
(April 2nd, 1995)

K. P. Jog
Shoun Hino

TABLE OF CONTENTS

ABBREVIATIONS

AnSS	Ānandāśrama Sanskrit Series
BS	*Brahmasūtra*
BSB	*Brahmasūtrabhāṣya* by Śaṅkara
BU	*Bṛhadāraṇyakopaniṣad*
BUB	*Bṛhadāraṇyakopaniṣadbhāṣya* by Śaṅkara
BUBV	*Bṛhadāraṇyakopaniṣadbhāṣyavārtika* by Sureśvara
CU	*Chāndogyopaniṣad*
NKL	*Nyāyakalpalatikā*
SP	*Śāstraprakāśikā* by Ānandagiri
SV	*Saṃbandhavārtika* by Sureśvara

INTRODUCTION

We have already stated in the Preface how BUBV 2.2 and 3 go merely to amplify, by adding explanatory details, the thought in BUBV 2.1. This becomes clear in the light of the synoptic contents of the two Brāhmaṇas under translation in this part of our work. (These are given below).

But first, it is necessary to record here that BUBV 2.1.20 stated that the vital force is a/the body, which is the Ātman— namely, the inner self— is the (basic or ultimate) truth of the *prāṇa*s 'organs' which are described as truth (Read: *etasmād ātmanaḥ sarve prāṇāḥ sarve lokāḥ sarve devāḥ sarvāṇi bhūtāni vyuccaranti ... prāṇā vai satyaṃ teṣām eṣa satyam*). Therefore, BU 2.2, which seeks to clarify the nature of the Ātman, i.e. the inner self, describes it figuratively as *śiśu* 'a young one' bound by physical bonds or, to speak precisely, the limiting adjuncts of the same. Also, it reveals the secret names of the Self. Naturally, therefore, BU 2.2 is called Śiśu Brāhmaṇa.

Then BU 2.3 goes to describe the two forms of the same Brahman (i.e. the inner self) in order to explain its secret names and its so-called composition which does not belie its description as the truth of the truth. The Brahman is here described as (i) having forms (*mūrta*) and (ii) not having any form whatever (*amūrta*). It (viz. which is *mūrta*) is then described as mortal (*martya*), limited in point of time and place (*sthita*), existent as distinct objects (*sat*) and finally that (*tyat*), viz. beyond description. The same is again described as comprising the perceptible (three in number) and imperceptible (two in number) elements (*bhūta*s). The *adhyātma* 'with reference to a/the body' and *adhidaivata* 'with reference to deities' forms also are well determined—this, in relation to three elements, viz. Pṛthivī, Ap and Tejas (*mūrta*) and that in relation to the remaining two elements, viz. Wind and Sky (*amūrta*). Finally, the form of that Puruṣa 'being' is revealed (with the help of examples) which leads to the proper philosophical and *true* description of its name also, and to the instruction (*ādeśa*) about its nature in the words *neti neti*. All this is significantly called Mūrtāmūrta Brāhmaṇa. This Brāhmaṇa, viz. 2.3, is comparatively longer than its preceding and, as a result, BUBV 2.2 is shorter than BUBV 2.3. This should become clear from the following synopsis of their contents.

BUBV 2.2:

In the beginning, Sureśvara brings out (in verses 1-7) how there is continuation of the thought of BUBV 2.1. Then he explains (in verses 8-15ab) the meaning of the *first section* of BUBV 2.2. He supplements to this explanation the interpretation of the word *sasthūṇam* offered by a pre-Śaṅkara Vedāntin Bhartṛprapañca (in verses 15cd-21). He explains the *second section* (in verses 22-24) and the *third section* (in verses 25-29). He explains the *fourth section* (in verses 30 and 31).

This shows how brief is Sureśvara's explanation of BUB. It is not necessary to present here the details of a comparative discussion about BUB and BUBV. It is necessary to point out, nevertheless, that Sureśvara avoids many of the details in BUB on *section four*. Possibly, he does not appear to notice any significant philosophical points revealed in them.

BUBV 2.3:

Sureśvara pays, it seems, greater attention to the introduction to the Brāhmaṇa (verses 1-14). He explains only minutely the purport of the *first section* (in verses 15-34) and thus clarifies the significance of the different concepts—or, rather, adjectives *mūrta*, *martya* etc.—in relation to the 'elements'. Then (in verses 35-44) he brings out, by way of explaining the words *mūrta*, *martya*, *sthita* and (finally) *sat* in relation to the three elements Pṛthivī etc. in the *second section*. He explains thereafter (in verses 45-48) the purport of the *third section*, stressing the meaning of Maṇḍala, i.e. Hiraṇyagarbha. Incidentally, following Śaṅkara's very briefly worded view of Bhartṛprapañca (in BUB) regarding the BU sentence *tyasya hy eṣa rasaḥ*, he presents the same (in verses 49-58ab) and then gives blame to it, by pointing out the faults involved in the same (in verses 58cd-68) at length; this is in relation to the deities connected therewith (*adhidaivata*).

Then he gives an exposition of *sections four* and *five* (in verses 69-82), i.e. of *mūrta* and *amūrta* in relation to a/the body (*adhyātma*) and the subtle (*amūrta*)— this includes Sureśvara's exposition of Bhartṛprapañca's opinion in this regard, for it is acceptable to him. After this, he finally brings out (in verses 83-89) in full the purport of *section six*, which needs, in agreement with Śaṅkara (BUB), and exhaustive treatment, and in greater details, of Bhartṛprapañca's theory related to the topic, viz. the form of that (i.e. immanent) Puruṣa in the shape of the inner self (verses 90-103), his own opinion on the same, as regards the faulty presentation of the relation of the sentence *tasya ha* ... to the context, viz. to the organs and impressions (verses 104-110); a full exposition of Bhartṛprapañca's notion about the entire theory (*prakriyā*) involved in this respect (verses 112-124) by pointing out in brief the faults, viz. its opposition to Vedic teachings and following inconsistently the views of Tārkikas (Sāṃkhyas included); and a fuller criticism of that theory (verses 125-137) which necessitates a refutation and rejection (also) of Bhartṛprapañca's postulation of the primordial matter as possessed of three *rāśi*s 'tendencies' (in verses 138-147). That is then followed by Sureśvara's own view on the meanings of the different words in the sentence *tasya ha* (verses 148-159).

He explains, in the course of his argument, the purport of the words *māhārajanaṃ vāsaḥ* (verses 160-170) and offers at length (in verses 171-213) his own opinion on the full import of the Vedāntic instruction *neti neti* and subsequently (in verses 214-235) states how that instruction is (more or less) a *vidhi*(*vākya*). Then, while concluding, he states the meaning of the BU statement *na hy etasmāt* (verses 236-243) and of the sentence *atha nāmadheyam* (verses 244-254). [His concluding remark in verse 254 is well summed up by NKL thus: *sopādhike brahmaṇi gṛhītasambandham padaṃ nirupādhikaṃ lakṣayatīty arthaḥ*.]

This statement of the synoptic contents of BUBV 2.2 and 3 (particularly those in BUBV 2.3) reveals how much importance Sureśvara attaches to the opinion of the great Vedāntic predecessor Bhartṛprapañca—this in relation to the interpretation of Vedāntic sentences in the light of his own theory of Bhedābheda. We preclude here any discussion on Bhartṛprapañca, since that forms an independent topic.

****

BṚHADĀRAṆYAKOPANIṢAD-BHĀṢYA-VĀRTIKA

2.2

Śiśu Brāhmaṇa

Sureśvara begins his discussion in BU 2.2 (basis of BUBV 2.2) with a brief statement regarding its relation to BU 2.1 (basis of BUBV 2.1). Yet that statement is too brief to convey fully (or properly) the import of Śaṅkara's comment on the relevant portion in BUB. Therefore we reproduce here BUB and add to it its English rendering. We hope that it should be useful in understanding Sureśvara's discussion better.

BUB reads (pp.295-297):

ब्रह्म ज्ञपयिष्यामीति प्रस्तुतम् । तत्र यतो जगज्जातं यन्मयं यस्मिंश्च लीयते तदेकं ब्रह्मेति ज्ञापितम् । किमात्मकं पुनस्तज्जगज्जायते लीयते च । पञ्चभूतात्मकम् । भूतानि च नामरूपात्मकानि । नामरूपे सत्यमिति ह्युक्तम् । तस्य सत्यस्य पञ्चभूतात्मकस्य सत्यं ब्रह्म । कथं पुनर्भूतानि सत्यमिति मूर्तामूर्तब्राह्मणम् । मूर्तामूर्तभूतात्मकत्वात्कार्यकरणात्मकानि भूतानि प्राणा अपि सत्यम् । तेषां कार्यकरणात्मकानां भूतानां सतत्त्वनिर्दिधारयिषया ब्राह्मणद्वयमारभ्यते सैवोपनिषद्व्याख्या । कार्यकरणसतत्त्वावधारणद्वारेण हि सत्यस्य सत्यं ब्रह्मावधार्यते । अत्रोक्तं प्राणा वै सत्यं तेषामेष सत्यम् इति । तत्र के प्राणाः कियत्यो वा प्राणविषया उपनिषदः का इति च ब्रह्मोपनिषत्प्रसङ्गेन करणानां प्राणानां स्वरूपमवधारयति । पथिगतकूपारामाद्यवधारणवत् ।

यो ह शिशुं साधानं सप्रत्याधानं सस्थूणं सदामं वेद तस्येदं फलम् । किं तत् । सप्त सप्तसंख्याकान्ह द्विषतो द्वेषकर्तॄन्भ्रातृव्यान्भ्रातृव्या हि द्विविधा भवन्ति द्विषन्तोऽद्विषन्तश्च । तत्र

द्विषन्तो ये भ्रातृव्यास्तान्द्विषतो भ्रातृव्यानवरुणद्धि । सप्त ये ये शीर्षण्याः प्राणा विषयोपलब्धिद्वाराणि तत्प्रभवा विषयरागाः सहजत्वाद्भ्रातृव्याः । ते ह्यस्य स्वात्मस्थां दृष्टिं विषयविषयां कुर्वन्ति तेन ते द्वेष्टारो भ्रातृव्याः । प्रत्यगात्मेक्षणप्रतिषेध-करत्वात् । काठके चोक्तम् अपराञ्चि खानि व्यतृणत्स्वयंभूस्-तस्मात्पराङ्पश्यति नान्तरात्मन् इत्यादि । तत्र यः शिश्वादीन्वेद तेषां याथात्म्यमवधारयति स एतान् भ्रातृव्यानवरुणद्ध्यपावृणोति विनाशयति ।

तस्मै फलश्रवणेनाभिमुखीभूतायाह । अयं वाव शिशुः । कोऽसौ । योऽयं मध्यमः प्राणः शरीरमध्ये यः प्राणो लिङ्गात्मा यः पञ्चधा शरीरमाविष्टो बृहन्पाण्डरवासः सोम राजन्नित्युक्तः । यस्मिन्वाङ्-मनःप्रभृतीनि करणानि विषक्तानि । पड्वीशशङ्कुनिदर्शनात् ।

(In the beginning, i.e. BU 2.1.15) it has been said, "I shall instruct you (as regards) the Brahman." And it has been instructed that "It is that single Brahman from which the world has originated, of what it is made and in what it (finally) merges." What then is the nature of that world (which) originates (from) and (finally) merges (in)? (The answer is:) It has the nature of the five (great) elements. And the elements have names and forms. (Again) it is (already) said (in the Śruti that) name(s) and form(s) are truth. The Brahman is the truth of the truth in the form of the five elements. (A question is asked:) How are the (five) elements truth? (In answer to this question is stated) the Mūrtāmūrta Brāhmaṇa. Owing to having the nature of the *mūrta* and *amūrta*, the (five) elements and the *prāṇa*s (organs in a/the body) also (come to) have the nature of causes and their means (and are therefore) truth (*satya*). Now begin the two Brāhmaṇas with a desire to determine the nature of those (five) elements which have the nature of causes and their means—that is the explanation of the Upaniṣad (viz. secret doctrinal teaching). Indeed, by determining the nature of causes and their means is determined the Brahman which is the truth of truth. In this regard, it is said, '*prāṇa*s are truth, this one (i.e. Prāṇa 'vital force') is their truth.

There, in that context (arise questions:) What are the *prāṇa*s? how many? and which are the Upaniṣads there that have (those) *prāṇa*s as the subject matter? (And this Upaniṣad, viz. BU) determines, while discussing the secret doctrine of the Brahman, the nature of (various) organs, the *prāṇa*s—this is like fixing the resting places on the path (of one's journey).

This (then) is the result (or gain) of (the statement) *yo ha vai śiśuṃ sādhānaṃ sapratyādhānaṃ sasthūṇaṃ sadāmaṃ veda*. What is that (exactly)? Seven, i.e. seven in number, inimical, i.e. haters, viz. the offspring of brothers—the offspring of brothers are of two types: (actual) haters and non-haters. Among them, those offspring of brothers who hate them (viz.) the haters does [the *śiśu* 'young one (of a cow)' kill (lit. check, or, restrain)]. Those which are the seven *prāṇa*s resting in the head, viz. the means (lit. openings) of securing (various) objects—from them are born attachments to (various) objects; these are for them the offspring of brothers (i.e. enemies), owing to their coming into existence together with them. Since they make (the Vital Breath's) eyes (lit. sight) prone towards the objects, therefore they are haters, the offspring of brothers (for them). (This is so) because they have the tendency (or, capacity) to hinder (or, prohibit) the inner self from realising (lit. seeing) the Ātman. In the *Kāṭhaka* (*Upaniṣad*), it is already said, "The self-born has cut away the different (lit. away from itself) organs; therefore, it sees outside [lit. away (from itself)] and not within its (own) self" and so on. In that case (that is to say,) when the existence of the offspring of brothers has been established, the one, who knows (about) the *śiśu* and others, and also determines (i.e. understands clearly) the true nature of them, restrains these offspring of brothers, i.e. overpowers them (and) destroys them.

To that one, who has become eager for (or, inclined to) hearing the result (of the *vidyā* 'knowledge about the Brahman'), the Upaniṣad says this (i.e. the following): "This is indeed the young (calf)." (The question is): 'Who is that?' That one is described as he, who is inside a/the body, the *madhyama* 'innermost' vital breath, that Vital Breath who is the subtle Ātman, the one who has occupied the body in five ways, the one who is great and clad in white robes, Soma, the king, the one in whom cling (various) organs, viz. speech (and) *manas* as the principal ones among them. This is clear from the example of pegs (serving as) fetters (on the feet) of a horse.

Here is stated the connection of 2.2 with the earlier portion of BU.

जगज्जनिस्थितिध्वंसा यस्मात्सिध्यन्ति तत्परम् ।
ब्रह्मेति प्राक्प्रतिज्ञाय यथावदुपदर्शितम् ॥१॥

Having first enunciated 'that it is the highest Brahman from which proceed the origin, sustenance and merger (lit. destruction) of the world', (that) was shown accordingly. [1]

This has, according to SP, reference to BU 2.1.20: *brahma te bravāṇi*. BUB states *brahma jñapayiṣyāmīti prastutam*. This refers to purport (=essence) of that sentence. The editor of NKL refers to 2.1.425 as indicative of this Brāhmaṇa.

तस्योपनिषदित्युक्तं तद्व्याख्यात्राधुनोच्यते ।
आ मैत्रेय्याः परब्रह्मसत्यस्य प्रतिपत्तये ॥२॥

(Also) it was stated 'This is the secret doctrine of the Upaniṣad'. And now is stated here full explanation of that [1] up to the (end of) Maitreyī (Brāhmaṇa), so that one should understand the truth, viz. the highest Brahman. [2]

This refers to BU 2.1.20; *tasyopaniṣat satyasya satyam iti* ....

[1]*tad = pratyagbrahma* (SP). But SP's remark does not appear consistent.

सृष्टिप्रस्ताव एतस्मिन्प्राणादेर्जन्म सूत्रितम् ।
यतोऽतः प्राणसंबन्धात्पूर्वं व्याख्या प्रपञ्च्यते ॥३॥

Since in this introductory statement regarding creation there has been enumerated the origin of Prāṇa etc., (therefore) from this[1] connection of Prāṇa (with the origin etc.) is now given in detail (its) explanation. [3]

SP points out that Śiśu Brāhmaṇa has the precedence over Mūrtāmūrta Brāhmaṇa (viz. 2.3).

[1]*ataḥ = etasmāt*; it is not an adverb in the sense of 'therefore'.

ततः परेण लोकादेरपि याथात्म्यमुच्यते ।
अध्यात्ममधिदैवं च देवताकरणाश्रयम् ॥४॥

Subsequent to that, there is stated the true nature of the world etc.[1] in relation to (both) the body and the gods in relation to[2] the deities and the organs. [4]

Here is given the reason as to why the Mūrtāmūrta Brāhmaṇa follows immediately after the Śiśu Brāhmaṇa.

[1]This refers to superintending god of the world.

[2]Or, depending upon.

प्राणादि सर्वमेवेदं पञ्चभूतसतत्त्वकम् ।
न हि भूतातिरेकेण प्रतीचः किंचिदिष्यते ॥५॥

Prāṇa etc., that is, all this is of the nature[1] of the five elements. Indeed nothing else than the elements is accepted to be existent beside the inner self.[2] [5]

The second line of the verse emphasises the idea that duality is conceived of only owing to ignorance about the true nature of the inner self.

[1]*satattva = svarūpa.*

[2]The inner self refers to the sentiency within (whereas the individual self is understood as a human being's self).

प्राणा वै सत्यमित्युक्तं के प्राणा इति यत्नतः ।
व्याख्यायन्तेऽथ ते प्राणास्तथोपनिषदश्च याः ॥६॥

It is (earlier) stated: 'Prāṇas are the truth.' Then those Prāṇas are explained with care (lit. purposefully) as an answer to the question 'which are those Prāṇas?' and also the secret doctrines of the same. [6]

प्राणेन मध्यमेनान्नं जग्धं वागादितर्पणम् ।
यथा करोति तद्वाच्यं प्राणोपनिषदश्च याः ॥७॥

Now is to be stated as to how the food eaten by the middle Prāṇa[1] effects pleasures of Vāk etc.; and also there are to be explained the secret doctrines of Prāṇa. [7]

[1]Supply: which moves in the mouth and nostrils. This refers to vital breath. SP explains this as *mukhanāsikāsañcārī prāṇaḥ*.

Now follows the discussion of BU 2.1.1.

यो ह वा इति प्रश्नोक्तिस्तस्यायमिति निर्णयः ।
शरीरेऽभ्याहितः प्राणो मूर्ध्नि प्रत्याहितस्तथा ॥८॥

The words *yo ha vai* ...[1] is the statement of the question about the Prāṇa and in the words *tasyāyam* ...[2] there is the decision (about it); Prāṇa resides[3] in the body and also resides specially in the head. [8]

[1]This introduces *yo ha vai śiśum ... sasthūṇaṃ* in the beginning of BU 2.2.1.

[2]It begins with *ayaṃ vā ... sthūṇānnaṃ dāma.*

[3]It literally means: is placed in ....

विषयेष्वनभिष्वङ्गाच्छिशुः प्राणोऽभिधीयते ।
वागादेरिव नासङ्गो यतः प्राणस्य विद्यते ॥९॥

Prāṇa is mentioned as young one of the animal because of its non-attachment to (various objects) of pleasure since Prāṇa does not have any attachment to them as Vāk etc. [9]

This verse states with reasons which justify the Śruti 'Prāṇa is Śiśu'. This indirectly reveals the nature of the section of Śiśu Brāhmaṇa.

शीर्षण्यप्राणसंस्था ये शब्दाद्या सङ्गलक्षणाः ।
भ्रातृव्यास्ते सहोत्पत्तेः प्रत्यग्दृष्टयपहारतः ॥१०॥

Those which are characterized as attachment to words etc. and are residing in Prāṇa in the head etc. are enemies,[1] since they are born together with Prāṇa—this is on account of the obscuring of knowledge about the individual self. [10]

[1]It literally means: born from (or, offspring of) a brother.

शरीरमस्याधानं स्याच्छरीरेऽवस्थितो यतः ।
सामान्यवृत्त्या प्राणोऽयं तस्मादाधानमुच्यते ॥११॥

The body is[1] the abode of this (Prāṇa), since (this one) has stayed in the body, performing[2] its common function; therefore (the body) is called the abode. [11]

In the *Sāṃkhyakārikā* there is mention of five different functions of the Wind with reference to different places in the body; and Prāṇa is called *sāmānyakaraṇavṛtti*. Cf. BUBV 1.5.

[1]*syāt* for *asti*.

[2]Literally, 'owing to the performance of'.

शरीराश्रयिणं प्राणं यतो वागादयः श्रिताः ।

अलं स्वकार्यनिष्पत्तौ न तु प्राणैकसंश्रिताः ॥१२॥

Since tongue[1] etc. has resorted to Prāṇa residing in the body, they are capable of accomplishing their own functions; but not so, if they have resorted to Prāṇa alone.[2] [12]

This is the statement of another reason for mentioning body as the abode of Prāṇa.

[1] Vāk here stands for the functioning organ, viz. tongue.

[2] This means that Prāṇa has no connection with the body: SP clarifies that in the case of stupor Prāṇa does not have any connection with the body and there is no functioning of organs. NKL refers to the sleep state and not stupor. Only in the waking state, Prāṇa is connected with the various organs which can function—in the v.l. of AnSS edition, the organs are described as *kāryakāraṇāni*. Read NKL: *dehaniṣṭhaprāṇāśritānāṃ tatsāmarthyāt* (i.e. *tattatkāryajananasāmarthyāt*— gloss in NKL edition) *prāṇasyādhānaṃ śarīram ity arthaḥ*.

प्रति प्रत्याहितत्वाच्च प्रत्याधानं शिरो विदुः ।
शिरोदेशविशेषेषु प्रति प्रति स आहितः ॥१३॥

They have known the head as the 'special abode', since (the prefix) *prati* is to indicate *pratyāhitatva* 'special placing (in every part of the body)'. (Indeed) that (*prāṇa*) is placed in each particular part of the head.[1] [13]

[1] The particular parts of the head are eyes, ears, nostrils and mouth. Deussen translates 'roof of the abode' for *deśa*.

अन्नपानसमुत्था हि शक्तिः प्राणो बलं तथा ।
बलावष्टम्भ एतस्मिन्प्राणो देहेऽवतिष्ठते ॥१४॥
अबल्यं नीत्वेति तथा प्राणोत्क्रान्तिः प्रवक्ष्यते ।

Indeed, power originates from food and drink; and (therefore) it is Prāṇa and also strength. Prāṇa stays in this body, viz. in this which has strength as its support. [14]

So also, the exit of Prāṇa (from the body) will be stated in the words *abalyaṃ nītvā* ... 'Having rendered it powerless .....'[1] [15ab]

The words *avaṣṭambha* and *avatiṣṭhate* refer to the word *sthūṇā* in BU. NKL connects this as *prāṇapadārtha* (=*prāṇāḥ sthūṇā ity āha prāṇapadasyārthaḥ*).

[1]Sureśvara, following Śaṅkara, is justifying the second line of verse 14 by the support of the Śruti statement *sa yatrā-yamātmābalyaṃ nyetya saṃmoham iva nyeti* (BU 4.4.1).

उच्छ्वासादिक्रियं केचिद्वायुं स्थूणां प्रचक्षते ॥१५॥

Some scholars[1] explain *sthūṇā* (the post) as the Wind which performs the activity of going out (of the body). [15cd]

Here Sureśvara, following Śaṅkara, refers to the view of Bhartṛprapañca regarding the strength of the body as the cause of Prāṇa. This shows how Sureśvara and Śaṅkara regardfully derive support from Bhartṛprapañca (possibly because of their agreement with him in respect of their use). SP appears to quote from Bhartṛprapañca thus *uktaṃ hi prāṇa ucchvāsaniḥśvāsakarmā vāyuḥ śarīraḥ śarīrapakṣapātī gṛhyate. etasyāṃ sthūṇāyāṃ śiśuḥ prāṇaḥ karaṇadevatāliṅgapakṣapātī gṛhyate. sa devaḥ prāṇa etasmin bāhye prāṇe saṃbaddha iti.*

[1]The plural is expressive of Sureśvara's respect for Bhartṛprapañca.

जाठराग्न्यभिसंबन्धाज्जग्धमन्नं त्रिधा क्रमात् ।
परिणामं व्रजत्येतत्स्थूलमध्यमसूक्ष्मतः ॥१६॥
स्थूलांशः पृथिवीमेति पुरीषं मूत्रमेव च ।
स्थूलदेहोपचित्यर्थो मध्यमोंऽशः प्रकीर्तितः ॥१७॥
यस्तु सूक्ष्मो रसोऽन्नस्य भागोऽमृतमितीर्यते ।
स हृद्देशं समागम्य नाडीमध्यसमाश्रयः ॥१८॥
हृदयाद्विप्रकीर्णाभिर्नाडीभिर्लिङ्गदेवताः ।

प्रीणयन्नुपचिन्वंश्च दामान्नमिति भण्यते ॥१९॥

On account of its connection with the fire in the stomach, this food which is eaten (by an individual) is transformed in three ways, respectively as of gross and middle size and as subtle in form. [16]
The gross portion becomes (*eti*) earth, faeces and urine; the portion of middle size is said to be effective in the increase of the gross body. [17]
And that which is the subtle (portion) of that food is that sap, called (also) *amṛta*. That (sap) reaches the region of the heart and, finding a place in the veins, [18]
(flowing) through various veins and from the heart, causes pleasure to the deities in subtle (form) and is therefore called the cord, the food (*dāmānna*).[1] [19]

These verses explain BUB *annaṃ dāma hi*, i.e. why food is called *dāman*.

देहं रसादिना बद्ध्वा सूक्ष्मांशेन शिशुं तथा ।
पाशद्वयाभिसंबन्धादन्नं दामेति शब्द्यते ॥२०॥

anna is called *dāman* on account of its close connection with two bonds;[1] viz. it has bound the body by the sap and also the young one (viz. Prāṇa) by the subtle portion (of the sap) etc.[2] [20]

This explains how food becomes *dāman* of various sizes.
[1]The *pāśadvaya* is for *deha* and *śiśu* (=Prāṇa).
[2]SP explains this as skin, flesh ....

दाम प्रतनुतां याति यदा कर्मक्षयात्तदा ।
यथास्वं यान्त्यथ प्राणा देहादुच्छिन्नबन्धनाः ॥२१॥

When the cord becomes very thin owing to the decrease (lit. destruction) in (effects of) *karman*, then the *prāṇas*, (organs) which have their bonds cut off, depart from the body in accordance with the nature of the deities associated with them. [21]

This verse states the relation between *dāman* and Prāṇa by the method of *anvayavyatireka*; the first line by *anvaya* and the second line by *vyatireka* method.

Now follows the discussion on BU 2.2.2.

प्रत्याधानसमूढस्य शिशोस्तस्यैव काश्चन ।
अक्षण्युपनिषदो वाच्यास्तमेता इत्यतः श्रुतिः ॥२२॥

Since some Upaniṣadic statements in relation to the eye (etc.) are to be stated with reference to that young one born as a consequence of its being supported, therefore there is the Śruti statement *tam etāḥ* .... [22]

उपासतेऽक्षणि प्राणं रुद्राद्याः सप्त देवताः ।
अक्षीणा इति ता ज्ञात्वा नान्नक्षयमुपाश्नुते ॥२३॥
मूर्ध्नि प्रत्याहितं प्राणमृषयः प्राणसंज्ञकाः ।
रुद्राद्या मध्यमं यस्मात्सततं पर्युपासते ॥२४॥

The seven gods [1] Rudra and others wait on [2] Prāṇa (residing) in the eye (etc.). Having known them as non-decreasing, [3] a worshipper does not experience decrease in (lit. destruction of) food, [23]
(since) [4] those seers, called Prāṇa, the seven gods Rudra and others ever particularly [5] wait upon that Prāṇa [6] which is supported in the head. [24]

Those seven gods related to the Śiśu under reference also become known as *prāṇa*s and seers. In the case of Rudra and others, we must remember that these are gods connected with seven particular parts of the head—not usual deities. We must also remember here how there is influence of ritualistic idea of differentiating a deity when it is related to one or another deity or thing. For example, Agni is different from Agni in *agnāviṣṇu*.

[1]Those are Rudra, Parjanya, Āditya, Agni, Indra, Pṛthivī and Dyau.

[2]*upāsate* literally meaning 'offer worship to'.

[3]Or, imperishable.

[4]NKL edition reads *yasmāt* which is better.

[5]Or, with great care/effort.

[6]This is *madhyama prāṇa*; cf. verse 7 above.

Now follows the discussion of BU 2.2.3.

अक्षण्येव यतः पूर्वं व्याख्यातो देवतागणः ।
श्रोत्रादिकरणार्थोऽयं श्लोकस्तस्मादुदाहृतः ॥२५॥

Because the group of gods in the eye (etc.) is enumerated already (i.e. in the second section), therefore this verse is now cited as conveying the meaning of the various (sense-) organs, ears etc.[1] [25]

This has a reference to the verse *arvāgbilaḥ* ... cited in BU with the words *tad eṣa śloko bhavati* (cf. *Śatapatha Brāhmaṇa* 14.5.2.4); cp *Atharvaveda* 10.8.9 (with variants). The verse is called *śloka* 'a non-Vedic metrical verse' though it is actually a Mantra 'Vedic verse'.

[1]Referring to the senses of seeing, hearing, smell, taste and touch.

विश्वरूपं यशो ज्ञेयं शब्दाद्यर्थावभासकम् ।
तेजस्तच्चाप्यनेकात्म विभिन्नार्थावभासनात् ॥२६॥

Fame of various kinds[1] is to be known as *tejas* 'light' which illuminates the objects, viz. wind etc. and that also is of various kinds since it reveals various objects. [26]

This explains the word *viśvarūpayaśas* in the Atharvavedic

Mantra. This refers to the deities other than Rudra etc. who are connected with other (sense-)organs. The objects illuminated by *tejas* are different and therefore *tejas* is said to have different kinds.

[1]It literally meas: having various forms/nature.

तीरे तस्यासते सप्त वायवः करणाश्रयाः ।
ऋषयश्च यशश्चेति प्राणा उक्तेन हेतुना ॥२७॥

On the brink of it (or, in the vicinity of it; this refers to *bila*) (in *arvāg*) sit seven Winds[1] residing in the organs;[2] (therefore) *prāṇas* are both the seers and the fame,[3] for the reason stated.[4] [27]

This explains the meaning of *tejas* in the Mantra cited.

[1]Sureśvara refers to the Wind. Possibly Sureśvara refers to the five sense-organs and *ucchvāsādi* in verse 15 above (read SP's citation: *uktaṃ hi prāṇa ucchvāsaniḥśvāsakarmā vāyuḥ śārīraḥ*; cited under verse 15 above).

[2]Cf. *devatākaraṇāśraya* in verse 4 above.

[3]SP states the gods are the seers because they act in relation to their objects (*spandātmakatva*) and they are fame because they reveal the nature of word etc. (*śabdādivyākhyānahetutva*).

[4]The explanation given by Śaṅkara of the reason is: because they are of the nature of activity (*spanda*).

वक्तृत्वात्तृत्वभेदेन वाग्द्विधैकैव भिद्यते ।
सप्तमी चाष्टमी चेति सैवैका प्रोच्यते ततः ॥२८॥

Vāk, which is only one, is described as twofold on account of the difference in its character as the speaker and as the eater and therefore that single one is called the seventh and the eighth (deity). [28]

This explains the Śruti's reference to Vāk in *vāgaṣṭamī brahmaṇā saṃvidānā*.

वर्णनिष्पादनं वाचा तथाद्यरसवेदनम् ।
भवेद्द्विकर्मसंयोगात्सप्तमी चाष्टमी च वाक् ॥२९॥

Revealing the utterance of a sound is accomplished (i.e. done) by Vāk and enjoyment of the sap is also (performed[1] by Vāk); and thus, owing to its connection with two activities, Vāk is the seventh and the eighth.[2] [29]

This verse further clarifies the thought of verse 28 above.
[1]Cf. SP: *rasavedanaṃ carvaṇakriyā.*
[2]Read NKL: *attṛtvena saptamī vaktṛtvena cāṣṭamīty arthaḥ.*

Now follows the discussion of BU 2.2.4.

विशिष्टाह्वानसिद्ध्यर्थमृषीणामुत्तरा श्रुतिः ।
इमावेवेति च तथा फलवत्स्यादुपासनम् ॥३०॥

Now, the subsequent Śruti statement *imāv eva* is for establishing the different, specific names of those seers and (with the intention that) the worship of those deities would be fruitful.[1] [30]

This discusses the passages *imāv eva ....*
[1]That is, for knowing the cause of their names.

सर्वस्येति फलोक्तिः स्यादुक्तोपासनकर्मणः ।
अन्नात्तृत्वनिषेधार्थं सर्वमस्येति भण्यते ॥३१॥

The word *sarvasya*[1] is for stating the result of the activity (or, activities) of the worship already mentioned and the words *sarvam asya*[1] are stated for the purpose of excluding the idea of the food as the enjoyer.[2] [31]

Here Sureśvara has in mind the notion in Saptānna Brāhmaṇa where *bhoktṛ* and *bhogya* interchange their positions.

[1]In the BU *sarvasyāttā bhavati sarvam asyānnaṃ bhavati ya evaṃ veda.*

[2]Read SP: *upāsitur yad bhojyaṃ* (or *bhogyaṃ*) *tasya taṃ prati na bhoktṛtvaṃ kiṃ tu bhogyatvam evety arthaḥ*; NKL has expressed the same idea in other words. This serves to exclude the idea of *sarvam eva* as a repetition of what is stated in *sarvasya.*

इति श्रीबृहदारण्यकोपनिषद्भाष्यवार्तिके द्वितीयाध्यायस्य
द्वितीयं ब्राह्मणम् ॥२॥

****

BṚHADĀRAṆYAKOPANIṢAD-
BHĀṢYA-VĀRTIKA
2.3
Mūrtāmūrta Brāhmaṇa

प्राणोपनिषदश्चोक्ताः प्राणाश्चापि समासतः ।
यत्तु तेषां परं सत्यं तदिदानीं निरूप्यते ॥१॥

(Earlier) the worships of (lit. secret doctrines about) Prāṇa are described and also (are described) Prāṇas, (both) in brief.[1] And (*tu*) what their ultimate truth is is now explained.[2] [1]

The word *upaniṣad*(s) refers to Upāsanā(s) of Rudra (and others) and the word *prāṇa* to (i) organs, and (ii) deities superintending over them.

[1]This is so because a full description would be too long owing to the largeness/infiniteness of the number of *prāṇa*s (SP).

[2]This is the purport of the present Brāhmaṇa.

प्राणाः किमात्मकास्तेषां कथं सत्यत्वमिष्यते ।
इत्येवमादि वक्तव्यमित्यर्थः पर आगमः ॥२॥

There is yet desired to be stated (i.e. needs) as to what the nature of (those) Prāṇas is and as to how the truth of them is understood (lit. accepted)—for stating this and other (related) matter (*ādi*) there follows the subsequent Śruti text. [2]

SP brings out the purpose of the beginning of this Brāhmaṇa even though it began as *dve vāva*, and not as *athāta ādeśaḥ* (*prāṇānām* ...). also, the purpose of *ity evam* is pointed out to refer to averting the doubt about the sentiency (or insentiency) of *prāṇa*s.

पञ्चभूतसतत्त्वानां शरीरकरणात्मनाम् ।
स्वरूपनिश्चयार्थाय प्रारब्धं ब्राह्मणं परम् ॥३॥

The subsequent Brāhmaṇa[1] is begun with the intention of the deciding nature of the body and the organs which are of the nature of five elements.[2] [3]

This verse further clarifies the idea of previous verse.

[1]That is, subsequent to Śiśu Brāhmaṇa. Yet SP refers only to the word *dve vāva*; read: *brāhmaṇaśabdas tadekadeśaviṣayaḥ.*

[2]*-bhūtasatattva=-bhūtātman* (SP).

यदुपाधिनिषेधोक्त्या नेतीति ब्रह्मणः स्फुटम् ।
आविश्चिकीर्षितं तत्त्वं तदेतदधुनोच्यते ॥४॥

Now is stated (in the following) that true nature of the Brahman which is desired to be clearly revealed in the words *neti* (and) the (various) adjuncts of which are rejected in the words (*neti* ...). [4]

Read NKL: *prakṛtabrahmanirūpaṇe prāṇanirūpaṇasya katham upayogaḥ*, as the reason for stating this verse.

स्वतोऽरूपं परं ब्रह्म तदविद्यादिहेतुतः ।
द्विरूपमिति निर्दिष्टं वियद्वत्कुम्भसंश्रयात् ॥५॥

The highest Brahman is by nature formless and yet, owing to ignorance etc.[1] (about the same), it is mentioned as having two forms—(this is) like (the sky) appearing twofold by its resorting to a pitcher.[2] [5]

This verse explains why the single Brahman is described to be twofold: *mūrta* and *amūrta* 'having a body and bodiless'.

[1]The word etc. refers to 'product of ignorance'.

[2]Though the sky is just one, it appears as one outside the pitcher and another contained in the pitcher (*ghaṭākāśa* and *bāhyākāśa*).

रूपे वा ब्रह्मणो विद्यान्मूर्तामूर्ते सवासने ।
ब्रह्मैव रूप्यते ताभ्यां ब्रह्मत्वं न हि रूपवत् ॥६॥

One should know that there are two forms of the Brahman: one with a body and one without it, together with their impressions[1]—by these two forms, the Brahman[1] is (fully) explained—for in reality the Brahman[2] does not possess any form. [6]

[1]The word *savāsane* qualifies the word *mūrtāmūrte* and excludes the idea of a third form of the Brahman.

[2]Sureśvara uses the word *brahmatva* as non-different from *brahman*; the suffix *tva* does not modify the sense of the word *brahman*.

अविद्यामात्रोपाध्येतद्ब्रह्म कारणमुच्यते ।
तदेव ज्ञातृतामेति बुद्ध्युपाधिसमाश्रयात् ॥७॥

The Brahman is said to be the cause, when it has the adjuncts,[1] viz. those (resulting from) ignorance alone; and that Brahman becomes the knower by resorting to the adjunct (of ignorance) called Buddhi.[2] [7]

This explains that the Brahman remains only one, even if it is named in two ways as the cause and the effect. Read NKL: *adhyastam ekaṃ rūpaṃ svarūpaṃ caikam(=cānyat) ityuktam.*

[1]These are various organs which have forms (i.e. are *mūrta*). They do not determine another *real* form of the Brahman, originate as they do in ignorance (*avidyā* regarding the Brahman).

[2]This also is an adjunct resulting from ignorance and having no form (*amūrta*).

तद्वृत्त्युपाधिसंस्थं सत्तज्ज्ञानमिति भण्यते ।
देवतेन्द्रियसंबन्धं तत्तत्तदभिधीयते ॥८॥

And that Brahman, appearing it its[1] functions, (viz. those resulting from) its limiting adjuncts, is called knowledge. And that is called by the name of (the organ), having relation to that organ and its god. [8]

Construe the second line thus *tad devatendriyasaṃbandhaṃ tad(=devatā) abhidhīyate*. Read SP: *tad eva cādhiṣṭheyopādhi tacchabdanirdeśyam ity arthaḥ*.

[1]This refers to Buddhi in the preceding verse and implies other organs as well.

तथा देहादिसंबन्धं दुःखजात्यादिमद्भवेत् ।
गोधनाद्यभिमान्येवं धनी गोमानितीर्यते ॥९॥

So also, that which has a connection with the body etc.,[1] comes to have misery, some genus etc.[2] (And) it is also said that one is possessed of the wealth, viz. cows, if (or when) one has the awareness of having the wealth of cows etc.[1] [9]

[1]The word etc. refers to different organ, gross and subtle.
[2]This refers to various shapes, names and so on.

अन्तर्यामी तथा साक्षी सर्वज्ञश्चेत्यविद्यया ।
मिथ्याध्यासैश्च तत्कार्यैरप्रमेयं प्रमीयते ॥१०॥

And that incomprehensible (Brahman) is comprehended as the one within and the witness and the omniscient—this owing to ignorance, false attributions and their[1] various effects. [10]

antaryāmin has reference to existence of the Brahman in a body, *sākṣin* to its being an agent in the action of knowing some objects and *sarvajña* to its knowing all that exists outside—all this is based on duality.

[1]SP refers *tat* to ignorance. But it is better to have ignorance and *mithyādhyāsa* as the meaning of that word.

एकं तावदिदं रूपं ब्रह्मणो मोहहेतुजम् ।

प्रत्यङ्मात्रैकधीगम्यं रूपं वास्तवमात्मनः ॥११॥

To begin with, one form of the Brahman is the product of delusion (and) the other form is understood from the knowledge of it, viz. as only that which exists within, (and) that is the true nature of the Ātman. [11]

In the first line, Sureśvara speaks of every object of our knowledge as a form the Brahman caused by false impression or ignorance. In the second line he refers to sentiency within a human body and therefore, it seems, he has used two different words *brahman* and *ātman* in the two different lines. He refers to the *adhyasta* and *vāstava* forms of the Brahman.

अव्यावृत्ताननुगतं द्वितीयासंभवादजम् ।
न वाक्यपदयोरर्थो भेदसामान्यवर्जनात् ॥१२॥

That Brahman is not distinguished from (any other objects) and it is not similar to any of them. It is unborn since there is no possibility of (existence of) a second (object). It is not some meaning to be conveyed by a sentence and/or a word since it precludes (both) difference and similarity. [12]

Hereby Sureśvara emphasises the indescribability of the Brahman.

न प्रमाणान्तरैर्गम्यं पराग्घेत्वसमन्वयात् ।
अनपेक्षितमात्रादि तदविद्यासमन्वयात् ॥१३॥

It is not to be understood by any of the means of knowing since it is not inseparably associated with the causes (of understanding) which are away from it;[1] it does not depend on[2] any means of knowing, because they are inseparably associated with ignorance. [13]

Sureśvara emphasises that the usual *pramāṇa-prameya-vyavahāra* is a product of ignorance, i.e. the absence of the knowledge of reality. SP refers to the SV which has discussed the impossibility of any relation of the Brahman with the various means of knowing; cf. SV 148ff.

[1]This refers to *pramāṇa* causing *pramā*.

[2]It literally means: 'it has no expectancy of'.

आत्मप्रत्ययमैकात्म्यं द्वितीयस्त्वात्मनो भवेत् ।
अनात्मप्रत्ययोऽतोऽहं स्वत एकोऽस्मि केवलः ॥१४॥

The uniqueness of the Ātman is from (i.e. results from) the realisation of one's own self, and any one who is really non-Ātman is other than the Ātman. Therefore, 'I am alone,' by myself (is the real knowledge). [14]

This implies the existence of the world as imaginary (i.e. false) like the serpent seen in a rope. The last part points to the nature of the Ātman as having no extension (*prapañca*) and no dependence on any other thing for its own existence.

Now begins the discussion of BU 2.3.1 up to verse 34.

यन्निषेधमुखेनेदं नेति नेतीति भण्यते ।
अविद्यामवधिं कृत्वा द्वे रूपे ब्रह्मणस्त्विमे ॥१५॥

These are the two forms of the Brahman which are denied in these words, viz. *neti neti*, which purport to negate (all duality), which keep in view ignorance in its full extent. [15]

It purports to say that one can mention the two forms only so long as ignorance persists and, on removal of ignorance, one cannot talk of any form of the Brahman.

अवधारणार्थ वावेति द्वे एवेति विनिश्चितौ ।
समुच्चिते सजातीयैरुत्तरैस्ते विशेषणैः ॥१६॥

The word *vāva* (in BU) is for emphasis and thus, when (the forms of the Brahman) are restricted as only two, they are connected[1] with the subsequent qualifiers (i.e. properties) born with them.[2] [16]

This is to explain the particles *vāva* and *ca*. The two particles *vāva* and (*dve*) *eva* together specify (or, define) the non-existence of any qualifier or attribute of the two, viz. *mūrta* and *amūrta*, forms of the Brahman. This is further clarified in the following verse.

[1]NKL paraphrases *samuccite* as *viśiṣṭe*.

[2]The moment we look upon the single Brahman as twofold, viz. *mūrta* and *amūrta*, the various qualifiers which follow can be postulated. The various adjectives are determined by the notion of duality arising out of the notion that this universe originates from the Ātman.

वावशब्दं चशब्देन प्रत्याहृत्याभिधीयते ।
मूर्तमेव च तद्रूपं ब्रह्मणोऽमूर्तमेव च ॥१७॥

The statement (in BU)[1] is made by putting together[2] the particle (lit. word) *vāva* with the particle *ca*. (Therefore, it means that the form of the Brahman is 'one having a body' and also 'one not having a body'. [17]

[1]Namely, *mūrtaṃ caivāmūrtaṃ ca*.

[2]This refers to BUB which paraphrases it as *mūrtaṃ caiva tathāmūrtaṃ cāmūrtam eva ca*. This means that Sureśvara explains away a doubt, '*nanv amūrtam eva ceti kathaṃ bhāṣyakārasyāmūrtaṃ cety atrāśruteḥ?*'

अविद्यावत्परं ब्रह्म मूर्तामूर्तादिलक्षणैः ।
विशिष्यते न धर्माणां मिथः संगतिरिष्यते ॥१८॥

The highest Brahman, (only when) associated with[1] ignorance is specified by the characteristics *mūrta*, *amūrta* etc.[2] but there is not accepted any connection of properties with one another. [18]

Sureśvara emphasises in this verse the real non-connection of the adjectives with the Brahman; in other words, he points to the *mithyādhyāsa* 'false association' of them with (i.e. superimposition on) the Brahman. Refer to BSB 3.2.6 which refers to the *mūrtāmūrtatva* of the Brahman.

[1]That is, overpowered by.

[2]The word etc. stands for *martya*, *amṛta*, *sthita*, *sat* and *tyat*.

विशेष्यार्थैकतन्त्रत्वाद्धर्माणां न परस्परम् ।
तथानपेक्षतस्तेषां संगतिः स्यात्कदाचन ॥१९॥

Since (any) properties are dependent only on the thing qualified (by them) there can never be their mutual connection; so also (there) cannot be connection among them, since they do not expect one another.[1] [19]

The adjectives *mūrta*, *martya*, *sthita* and *sat* refer to various *dharmas* (=*guṇas*) of the Brahman (of course, due to *avidyā*) and they do not get connected with one another. SP points out that, as in the *aruṇādhirakaṇa* of *Mīmāṃsāsūtra* 3.1.6.12 which refers to *aruṇa* (=*guṇa*) of 'cow' (a *dravya* that is *guṇin*), these *dharmas* do not necessarily stand in connection (*saṃgati*). This is implied in the second line of this verse.

[1]This is for *anapekṣataḥ* which is *anapekṣatvataḥ*. Cf. verse 13cd above and note thereon.

विज्ञानपुरुषान्तस्य ब्रह्मणः परमात्मनः ।
तमस्विनोऽथ द्वे रूपे तदन्याव्यतिरेकतः ॥२०॥

Thus then there are two forms of the highest Ātman, i.e. the Brahman, which ends in the knowing self[1] (and) which is overpowered by darkness,[2] there is no separate existence of any one other than that. [20]

[1]This refers to the most minute, yet perceptible, form of the

Brahman, maybe, Hiraṇyagarbha which appears to create the world—cf. NKL: *sṛṣṭyanantaraṃ praviṣṭasya.*

[2]This is literal translation of *tamasvin* which means 'possessed of'.

क्लृप्तसर्पादिभिर्यद्वदज्ञातायाः स्रजः सदा ।
वास्तवोऽवास्तवो वा न व्यतिरेको न चान्वयः ॥२१॥
तद्वन्न व्यतिरेकेण ब्रह्मणो द्वे स्वतः सदा ।
नापि चाव्यतिरेकेण ते तु ब्रह्मैव निर्द्वयम् ॥२२॥

As, on account of a serpent etc.[1] which are imagined (in the place) of wreathe (etc.),[2] there is no real or unreal (thing which exists) beside it, or there is no connection (of the same with another), [21]
in the same way, the two (forms) of the Brahman (do) not (exist) as apart from itself or as (connected) with it; the two are just the Brahman which is free from (i.e. devoid of) duality.[3] [22]

[1]The word etc. implies other examples of misapprehension (*adhyastakalpanā*) such as *śuktikārajata*, (*ekaś*) *candraḥ sadvitīyaḥ*.

[2]Though only *śrak* is mentioned, the other objects, viz. *śuktikā* and (*eka*) *candra* are implied.

[3]Read SP: *bhāsamānayor* [*mūrtāmūrtayor*] *dvayoḥ kā gatir ity āśaṅkyāha te tv iti*.

अण्वाद्यवयवं मूर्तं पीनं संस्थानवद्दृढम् ।
तद्विरुद्धममूर्तं स्यान्निरंशं देशवन्न च ॥२३॥

'That which has a form' if made up of parts, viz. *aṇu* etc., solid and firm like a composition and (that which is) 'not having a form' is opposed to it (in nature),[1] i.e. partless and undivided into regions. [23]

This refers to the twofold objects, viz. (i) the earth, waters and fire as having parts and regions and (ii) the Wind and

Sky as not having them.

[1]Here *tadviruddham* means *apīna* and *adṛḍha*.

मर्त्यं मरणधर्मि स्याद्यद्विनश्वरलक्षणम् ।
अमृतं तद्विरुद्धं च ध्रुवं यन्न विपद्यते ॥२४॥

Mortal is what is liable to perishing;[1] it is characterized as not abiding (for ever). Immortal is what is opposed to it;[2] it is permanent and does not come to destruction. [24]

This explains the meaning of the word *martya*.

[1]It literally means: what has the property of decay or death.

[2]Namely, the mortal.

आश्रितं स्थितमत्र स्याद्गत्वाऽव्याप्य च तिष्ठति ।
तद्विरुद्धं तथा यत्स्यादेत्येव न तु तिष्ठति ॥२५॥

The word *sthita* here[1] means that which is supported (in some place); and that goes (to some place) and stays on it without having pervaded it and that, which is opposed to that, goes (to some place) but does not stay there. [25]

This explains *sthitaṃ ca* ....

[1]That is, in this BU sentence.

सदिति व्यक्तरूपं यद्गृह्यमाणविशेषणम् ।
प्रत्यक्षं तद्विरुद्धं त्यदप्रत्यक्षं तथोच्यते ॥२६॥

The word *sat* means (having) a manifest form whose qualifiers can be grasped and it is directly perceptible and what is opposed to that is then called *tyat*, it is described as what is not directly perceptible. [26]

This brings out the purport of *sat*.

क्षितिर्जलं तथा वह्निरित्येतन्मूर्तमुच्यते ।
भूतद्वयममूर्तं च वायुश्चाकाशमेव च ॥२७॥

The earth, waters and also fire are this (Brahman) which is said to have a form and the two elements, the Wind and Sky are (the Brahman) which does not have a form. [27]

This refers to the five great elements divided into two groups, *mūrta* and *amūrta*.

मूर्तं मर्त्यं स्थितं सच्च क्षित्यबग्नित्रयं विदुः ।
अमूर्तामृतयत्त्यत्तु वाय्वाकाशद्वयं स्मृतम् ॥२८॥
मूर्तत्वादेव मर्त्यं तन्मर्त्यत्वादेव तत्स्थितम् ।
स्थितत्वादिन्द्रियग्राह्यं निर्धार्येदंतया पृथक् ॥२९॥
सोपाख्यत्वान्न तद्व्यापि क्वचिदेकांशवत्स्थितेः ।
स्थितत्वाच्चापि तन्मर्त्यं मर्त्यत्वान्मूर्तमेव च ॥३०॥
अमूर्तत्वादमर्त्यं तद्यद्व्यापि त्यदतीन्द्रियम् ।
अतीन्द्रियत्वात्तद्व्यापि व्यापित्वाच्चामृतं ततः ॥३१॥
अस्थितत्वादमूर्तं तदाकारव्यक्तिवर्जितं ।
हेतुतत्फलरूपेण मूर्तादेः संगतिर्मिथः ॥३२॥

They have known the triad of the earth, waters and fire as having a form, mortal, limited and existing (i.e. directly perceptible) as not having a form, and the two, viz. Wind and Sky are known immortal, moving and that (beyond direct perception).[1] [28]

Only since it has a form, it is mortal,[2] and only since it is mortal, it is said to be steady (i.e. limited for some time). And because it is steady, it can be grasped by the sense-organs after determining it as 'this is distinct from others'. [29]

(And) since that has a name, it is not pervasive; because it stays at some place like a part (of it) and because it has (so) stayed, it is mortal. And because it is mortal, it is possessed of a form. [30]

Since it does not have a form[3] it is immortal and that which is pervasive, it is 'that,' i.e. beyond sense-organs. Because it is beyond sense-organs, it is pervasive; and because it is pervasive it is immortal. [31]

Because it is not steady (i.e. limited for some time), it is without a form and any manifestation of shape—thus the properties *mūrta* etc.[4] having relations in the form of the cause and the effect stand (i.e. are) mutually connected. [32]

[1]Cf. *tyad apratyakṣam* in verse 26 above.

[2]In these two verses, viz. 29 and 30, Sureśvara explains how the adjectives *mūrta*, *martya* etc. give rise to every subsequent adjective and *vice-versa*.

[3]This and the next verse state the same adjectives (as described in the two preceding verses) and help to bring out clearly the cause and relation among them.

[4]The word etc. refers to *martya*, *sthita* and *sat*.

अक्षसूत्रवदन्योन्यं सामर्थ्यस्याप्रहाणतः ।
हेतुतद्वत्तया ज्ञेयामूर्तादेरपि संगतिः ॥३३॥

Because there is no loss of the capacity (among those, viz. that having a form etc. to modify one another) as in the case of the beads and the thread (in a rosary); in the same way, it should be known that what has not a form etc.[1] is (to be understood as) connected in the form of the cause and its effect.[2] [33]

[1]The word etc. stands for *amṛta*, *asthita* and *asat*.

[2]It literally means: that which has that, viz. that cause.

संभवेऽन्यतमस्यापि सर्वेषां संभवो यतः ।
अतोऽवधारणार्थाय तत्रैवग्रहणं कृतम् ॥३४॥

Since all of these come into existence immediately as any one of them comes into existence, therefore, for the sake of emphasis, there is the insertion of the word *eva*.[1] [34]

[1]Cf. *eva* in verse 29 above, viz. *mūrtatvād eva* and *amūrtatvād eva*.

Now follows the discussion on BU 2.3.2 up to verse 44.

तयोरुद्दिष्टयोर्मूर्तं प्रथमं तावदुच्यते ।
अन्यद्वाय्वन्तरिक्षाभ्यां भूतत्रयमिहोच्यते ॥३५॥

To begin with there is first explained, that one of the two thus enumerated which has a form and thus here[1] is explained that triad of elements which is other than the Wind and Sky. [35]

This explains *etan mūrtam* ....

[1]That is, in verses 36-38 which follow.

मूर्तं संस्थानवद्ध्येतत्तथा मर्त्यं विनाशवत् ।
एतत्स्थितं परिच्छिन्नमेतत्सत्सविशेषणम् ॥३६॥

This one, which has a form, is in the form of construct and also that is mortal, viz. it is perishable; this has stayed (for some time), i.e. is limited (or measured by another object) and this is existent, i.e. it is having attributes. [36]

This explains *etan martyam* ....

चतुर्विशेषणस्यास्य क्षित्यबग्न्यात्मकस्य हि ।
चतुष्टयरसत्वार्थं पुनरुच्चारणं कृतं ॥३७॥

Indeed of this one, which has these four attributes, viz. of what is of the nature of the earth, waters and fire, is stated once again with a view to conveying that 'the group of the four'[1] are the essence (of them). [37]

This explains *tasyaitasya* .... This means that the four adjectives qualify (are the effects of—Naiyāyikas terminology) all the three elements. It is not intended to qualify (only) one of them (at one time). Further, the statement of the four, *mūrta* etc., once again—immediately after verse 36—is not to be considered as repetition—so it is intended. Cf. NKL: *adhikavacanam anyārthaṃ dyotayatīty arthaḥ.*

[1]*mūrta*, *martya*, *sthita* and *sat*.

सर्वव्यापी रसो ह्येष शश्वत्तपति यो रविः ।
चतुष्टयान्वयादेष भूतत्रयरसः स्मृतः ॥३८॥

Indeed this sun who ever shines (lit. heats) is the all-pervasive essence; since it is connected with 'the group of the four'.[1] This is known as the essence of the three elements. [38]

This explains the meaning of *sa eṣa tapati.*

[1]This is because the sun makes this division visible.

य एष तपतीत्यत्र मण्डलं परिगृह्यते ।
चतुष्टयं हि मूर्तादि मण्डले गृह्यते यतः ॥३९॥

Here, in the BU sentence *sa eṣa tapati* is understood the orb (of the sun), because 'the group of the four', viz. *mūrta* etc., is grasped while there is the orb shining. [39]

This explains the meaning of *eṣa* as standing for the orb of the sun, not any live being.

चतुर्णामन्वयो हीति हेतुनात्रविभाव्यते ।
सतश्च ग्रहणं विद्याच्चतुर्णामुपलक्षणम् ॥४०॥

By the word *hi* which is (expressive of) the reason in this (statement) is understood the association of 'the group of the four' and (therefore) one should understand (here) the inclusion of *sat* as indicative of[2] 'the group of the four'. [40]

[1]This explains the significance of the word *hi* in *sato hi.*

[2]Read NKL: (*sato hi iti*) *etat caturṇāṃ madhye anuktānām mūrtādīnam upalakṣaṇam ity arthaḥ.*

कृष्णसारं यथा स्थानं चक्षुषः करणात्मनः ।

तथा हिरण्यगर्भस्य मण्डलं करणात्मनः ॥४१॥

As in the case of the eye, which has the nature of a sense-organ, the dark pupil is its abode,[1] so is orb the abode of Hiraṇyagarbha that has the nature of sense-organs. [41]

[1]The words *sthāna* and *maṇḍalam* are synonymous.

उत्सर्गाद्रूपनिर्माणे प्राधान्यं तेजसो यतः ।
तस्माद्रसत्वनिर्देशः क्रियते मण्डलात्मनि ॥४२॥

Since, in the act of the creation of various forms (in the universe), prominence belongs to *tejas*,[1] there is reference made here to the character of the orb as the essence. [42]

This explains why there is mentioned the orb of the sun instead of *tejas*.

[1]Cf. BU 1.2.2: *tejo raso nirvartata*. Also, cf. verse 44 below.

अप्क्लिन्नः पार्थिवो धातुस्तेजसा परिपच्यते ।
अङ्कुराद्यभिनिष्पत्तौ मुख्यतैवं हि तेजसः ॥४३॥

Indeed prominence is given to *tejas* which is thus understood since at the time of (the appearance) of the sprout there appears heating (lit. waking) of the earthly element[1] which is wetted by water. [43]

[1]It refers to the softness created in earth or seed by water; cf. SP: *adbhir vikledaṃ mṛdutvam āpāditaḥ śālyādiḥ pṛthivī-svabhāvaḥ*.... This justifies the *prādhānya* of *tejas* (in *rūpasarga*).

सारस्त्रयाणां भूतानां रसो मण्डलमुच्यते ।
एतत्साराणि हि त्रीणि भूतान्याहुर्विपश्चितः ॥४४॥

The essence of the three elements (viz. earth, waters and fire) is called the orb; indeed the wise ones have declared that these three elements have this as their essence. [44]

This explains BUB *trayāṇāṃ hi* ... which gives yet one more reason (viz. *vidvatprasiddhi*) as to why the *maṇḍala* is held to be *bhūtatrayasāra*.

Now follows the discussion of BU 2.3.3 up to verse 68c.

मण्डलायतने यत्तु कारणं संश्रितं विभोः ।
विराजो देवदेवस्य तदिदानीमिहोच्यते ॥४५॥

What in the abode of this orb has been accepted (i.e. stated)[1] as the cause pertains to the all-pervasive Virāj,[2] the lord of the gods—(how) that (is) is now explained here (i.e. in what follows). [45]

[1]The v.l. in AnSS edition *saṃsthitam* 'has remained' does not appear convincing.

[2]Virāj is for Hiraṇyagarbha, Sūtra, *kaliṅga* (in verse 47 below).

आदित्यान्तर्गतः साक्षात्करणात्माभिधीयते ।
वाय्वाकाशरसत्वेन तत्रामूर्तान्वयो यतः ॥४६॥

The one who is inside the sun is called the Ātman of the different organs of perception since therein is the presence of the one which does 'not have a form'[1] as the essence of the Wind and Sky. [46]

[1]Read SP: *amūrtagrahaṇam amṛtāditrayopalakṣaṇam*.

कलिङ्गारम्भसिद्ध्यर्थं वाय्वाकाशसमुद्भवः ।
ईश्वरात्कारणाद्यस्माल्लिङ्गं तेन रसस्तयोः ॥४७॥

Since the origin of the Wind and Sky is from the cause, viz. the Lord, for effecting the activity of the various organs, viz. *ka*,[1] he is the *liṅga* and essence of the two.[2] [47]

Here Sureśvara seems to be borrowing the idea of Sāṃkhyas about *liṅga*, inferred sentience in a body.

[1]This stands for Sūtrātman or Hiraṇyagarbha. Here Sureśvara uses an unusual word *ka-liṅga*.

[2]The Wind and Sky are thus subordinate to *liṅga*, viz. Virāj.

वाय्वाकाशरसो ह्येष इति हेतुः प्रदर्श्यते ।
त्यस्य ह्येष रस इति यथोक्तो मण्डलात्मनि ॥४८॥

Now is stated the reason as to why this one is (described as) the essence of the Wind and Sky. This is so said in the statement *tyasya hy eṣa rasaḥ* with reference to the Ātman in the orb. [48]

This explains *asya hi*. In verses 45ff. Sureśvara holds Hiraṇyagarbha (*liṅga*), and the knower of the field (as well) as synonymous with sentient being in the orb of the sun; cf. *ādityāntargataḥ* in verse 46 above.

हिरण्यगर्भक्षेत्रज्ञं रसं केचित्प्रचक्षते ।
कारणं रसशब्देन यस्मादत्राभिधीयते ॥४९॥

Some scholars hold (lit. say) that Hiraṇyagarbha, the knower of the field, is the essence, since in the cause[1] is expressed by the word *rasa*. [49]

This explanation is offered by Bhartṛprapañca; it is stated in verses 49 to 57ab. Read SP with advantage: *tyasya hītyādau rasaśabdena bhūtadvayakāraṇam uktaṃ na ca tac cetanād anyan na ca jīvas tathāsāmarthyān nāpi paraḥ kauṭasthyāt tasmāc cetanaḥ sūtrakṣetrajño 'tra rasa ity arthaḥ*. Both Śaṅkara and Sureśvara mention this with some explanations.

[1]This means: the origin.

यस्माद्धिरण्यगर्भस्य कर्म वाय्वन्तरिक्षयोः ।
प्रयोक्त्रव्यक्तयोस्तस्माद्रसः क्षेत्रज्ञ उच्यते ॥५०॥

Since the activity of Hiraṇyagarbha is the impeller in the case of the two 'not directly perceptible'[1] Wind and Sky, the knower of the field is said to be their essence. [50]

This clarifies why Hiraṇyagarbha is the *kāraṇa*.
[1]AnSS edition has a v.l. in the second line, viz. *prayoktṛ-vyaktayoḥ*, but that being a Dvandva compound, does not *properly* qualify *vāyvantarikṣayoḥ*— indeed, an inferior reading.

भूतद्वयरसो ज्ञेयो मण्डले चेतनः पुमान् ।
त्यस्य ह्येष रस इति तत्सिद्धौ कारणाभिधा ॥५१॥

The sentient man in the orb (of the sun) is to be understood as the essence of the two elements[1] and the statement of the reason for effecting this is in the words *tyasya hy eṣa rasaḥ*. [51]

This is a brief statement of the sentence *tasyaitasyāmūrtasya*; it justifies the argument in the preceding verse.
[1]This is a reference to the Wind and Sky.

न्यायोक्तेरेव संसिद्धेः प्रतिज्ञातस्य वस्तुनः ।
क्षेत्रज्ञः कारणं कस्मादित्यत्र न्याय उच्यते ॥५२॥

Since what is enunciated becomes established by the statement of the reason, here[1] is stated the (logical) reason as to why the knower of the field is the cause. [52]

The statement of the reason (*nyāya*) is for averting a doubt about the uselessness of it which is implied in the Śruti statement (*nyāya*).
[1]In the sentence *tyasya hy eṣa rasaḥ*.

एतस्मिन्मण्डले योऽन्तर्विज्ञानात्मत्वमागतः ।
अविद्याभावनाकर्महेतुतो नान्यकारणात् ॥५३॥

He who has become the inner self in this orb of the sun has become so only because of (his) activity which proceeded from ignorance; and not from any other motive. [53]

SP points out that Sureśvara states the reason for establishing the statement of the Śruti in the common or popular way of *nyāya* 'reasoning'. Further, it seems to quote Bhartṛprapañca's statement: *nyāyam eva darśayan yo hy etasmin maṇḍale vijñātmeti.* Translation of *avidyābhāvanākarma* ... is not certain/correct!

तस्य यत्कर्मरूपं तद्वियद्वायुप्रयोजकम् ।
खस्थस्य कर्मणस्तस्य मरुत्प्रस्पन्दरूपिणः ॥५४॥
वाय्वाकाशप्रनाड्यैवं तेजसः संभवस्ततः ।
जज्ञाते तेजसो भूते जलं च पृथिवी तथा ॥५५॥

And that which has the nature (lit. form) of his activity is the cause (of the origin) of the Wind and Sky—that is the activity of him who stays in the sky and has the form of the flutter of the wind. [54]
Thus there is then the origin of *tejas* through the channels of the Wind and Sky and from that *tejas* were born the two elements water and earth. [55]

We read the second line of verse 54 as *khasthasya karmaṇas tasya*, following the NKL edition.
On verse 55 refer to verse 42 above. Also read SP: *tat* (=standing for *karmarūpam* in verse 54) *ākāśam utpādya tadrūpeṇa sthitaṃ tasya marut kāryaṃ tena spandātmanā sthitasya dvayadvārā teja evaṃ karmaṇas tayos tejasaś ca janmety arthaḥ.* The meaning of *taijase itare bhūte* is given in *jajñāte* ....

कर्मणा पौरुषेणैवं रसभूतेन संभवः ।
वाय्वन्तरिक्षयोर्यस्माद्रसस्तेन पुमांस्तयोः ॥५६॥

Since thus there is the origin of the Wind and Sky from the activity belonging to the man,[1] which has become the essence, the man (in the orb of the sun) is the essence. [56]

This is the concluding remark in the view of Bhartṛprapañca.
[1]This man is Hiraṇyagarbha.

मेधया तपसेत्यादि तथा च प्रागुदाहृतम् ।
न्यायेनानेन पुरुषो रसशब्देन भण्यते ॥५७॥

So has it been stated earlier in the words *medhayā tapasā* (*'janayat*) [1] and for this reason is that man mentioned by the word *rasa*. [57]

There is cited here an authority from Śruti to support the statement in the preceding verse.

[1] BU 1.5.1.

त्यस्य ह्येष इति ह्युक्त्या न्यायः श्रुत्यायमुच्यते ।

In the words *tyasya hy eṣa rasaḥ* is stated by the Śruti the reason.[1] [58ab]

[1] Cf. verse 51cd and 52 above.

Now follows, in verses 58cd-68, arguments against the view of Bhartṛprapañca.

नैतदेवं भवेन्मर्तरसेनास्यासमत्वतः ॥५८॥
भूतत्रयस्य मूर्तस्य रसो मण्डलमभ्यधाः ।
धर्मैश्चतुर्भिर्मूर्ताद्यैर्भूतत्रयवदन्वितम् ॥५९॥
अमूर्तयोरपि रसो लिङ्गात्मा गृह्यतां तथा ॥६०॥

This cannot be so, since this will result in the inequality of this essence (of what does not have a form) with the essence of what has a form. [58cd]
You have called the essence of the triad of elements, which has a form, by the name *maṇḍala* and which is connected with (i.e. possessed of) the four properties, *mūrta* etc. in the same way as the three elements. [59]
Therefore, the essence of even the two (elements), which do not have a form, is to be understood as the nature of *liṅga* [1]

'subtle form'. [60]

In verse 58cd above, argument is made about the inequality which is clarified here: In the view of Bhartṛprapañca, the essence of the three elements which have a form is the orb of the sun (which is gross) and the essence of the Wind and of the Sky is not a subtle body; but it is the knower of the field, a sentient being. Here, Sureśvara addresses the first line of verse 59 directly to Bhartṛprapañca—this is clear from the reading *abhyadhāḥ* in verse 49b, against the v.l. noted in AnSS edition *abhyadhāt*.

[1]*liṅga* is the subtle form (of a living being).

वाक्यप्रवृत्तेस्तुल्यत्वान्न युक्तोऽत्रान्यथाग्रहः ।
वैरूप्यलक्षणो दोषः सत्येवं वः प्रसज्यते ॥६१॥

Since the procedure of the Vedic sentence in either case is similar, it is not proper to adopt a different procedure (in the sentence referring to *amūrtarasa*). (For) if this is so, there would necessarily result a fault of accepting dissimilarity (of procedures) in the two sentences. [61]

This verse gives reason for blaming Bhartṛprapañca for his aforesaid view.

In these verses Sureśvara is putting forth the argument of Śaṅkara cryptically. Śaṅkara's argument is: The three elements which have a form have an essence (or, cause) that has a form, so also the two elements which do not have a form have an essence (or, cause)–cf. verse 63 below–which has a form. So far, this is agreeable, but Bhartṛprapañca holds that, in the first case, the essence (or, cause)–cf. verse 63 below–is non-sentient and, in the other, sentient. This results into dissimilarity. This is objectionable.

अथ मूर्तरसोक्त्यापि चेतनस्यैव चेद्ग्रहः ।
अत्यल्पं भवताभाणि सर्वमात्मैव नो यतः ॥६२॥

If (Bhartṛprapañca might argue) it is held that in the statement about the essence (or, cause)–cf. verse 63 below–of what has a form is only a sentient being, (then Śaṅkara's answer is:) Oh. You have said just a small (i.e. insignificant, or unnecessary) thing, since we have accepted that all this is but the Ātman. [62]

Śaṅkara thinks all that effort of Bhartṛprapañca is not necessary in view of the accepted doctrine of Vedānta (according to Śaṅkara) that, in the final analysis, every effect is but caused by the Ātman (just through ignorance).

न ह्यात्मव्यतिरेकेण किंचित्कारणमिष्यते ।
तेन तेन स्वरूपेण प्रत्यगात्मैव कारणम् ॥६३॥

Indeed there is not accepted any thing other than the Ātman as the cause (for the effects)[1] since it is only the inner self in one form or another which is the cause.[2] [63]

Read SP (which brings out the purport of this verse): *parasyaivājñātasya kāraṇatāyā vaidikatvād ity arthaḥ.*

[1]Here, there is reference to the elements and their modifications.

[2]This sets aside the notion of Kṣetrajña (i.e. a particular Jīva).

मण्डलात्मनि चाधारे लिङ्गात्मैवावसीयताम् ।
करणस्यैव तत्स्थत्वाद्विज्ञानात्मा हि लिङ्गगः ॥६४॥

And let it be understood that there is the subtle Ātman at the basis of what has the nature of an orb, because it is the inner self[1] which exists in the subtle body for the organs rest (i.e. are supported) in the same.[2] [64]

[1]This is for Vijñānātman already referred to in verse 53 above. It is the same as Jīva.

[2]That is, Kṣetrajña.

अज्ञातः पुरुषो यस्मात्कार्यकारणशब्दभाक् ।

अज्ञातमिथ्याविज्ञानरूपत्वान्न तु तत्त्वतः ॥६५॥

(This is so) because Puruṣa is not known as designated by the words cause and effect; it is so (i.e. *kāryakāraṇabhāk*), because of its nature which is not known and has some false notion about it; it is not (indeed) that in reality. [65]

In the argument, there is stress laid on the cause and effect relation. The two must be similar, while Bhartṛprapañca seems to accept this cause and effect relation, whereas Śaṅkara does not accept it.

अचेतनेषु लोकेऽस्मिन्न दृष्टा पुरुषाभिधा ।
इति चेन्नैतदेवं स्यादचित्केष्वपि दर्शनात् ॥६६॥
त एतान्सप्त पुरुषानित्यादिश्रुतिवाक्यतः ।
असंवित्केऽपि पक्षादौ दृश्यते पुरुषाभिधा ॥६७॥

(Indeed) there is nowhere noticed in the world the use of the word *puruṣa* in the case of the non-sentient (things). (Yet an objection can be raised:) No, this is not so, since it is noticed in the case of those which are of the nature of the non-sentient. [66]
[Thus it is learnt (i.e. known)] from the Śruti statement *ta etān sapta puruṣān* ...,[1] and also in the case of the parts (of the beings' bodies)[2] etc.; which do not have any sentience, there is the designation (for them) Puruṣa. [67]

Verse 67 explains the thought in verse 66.

[1]Read SP and NKL: *te prāṇā na śaktā vibhaktā* (not in NKL) *vyavahāraṃ janayituṃ* (NKL: *darśayitum*) *iti kṛtālocanās tvakcakṣuḥśrotrajihvāghrāṇavāṅmanorūpān etān puruṣān ekaṃ liṅgātmakaṃ* (NKL: *liṅgaṃ*) *puruṣam akurvan* (untraceable!) and also *sa vā eṣa puruṣo 'nnarasamayaḥ* (*Taittirīyopaniṣad* 2.1).

[2]Cf. SP: *pakṣādau tadavayavabhākṣu kośeṣu iti yāvat* and NKL: *pakṣapucchādeḥ samūhe kośe ity arthaḥ*.

अध्यात्मोक्त्यवधिज्ञप्त्या अधिदैवतकीर्तनम् ।
मूर्तामूर्तविभागोऽयमध्यात्ममधुनोच्यते ॥६८॥

(Now) by informing about the beginning of the discussion on what pertains (or, belongs) to the body,[1] there is (completion of) the statement[2] of what pertains to the deities (in the body). Now (then) follows the division of *mūrta* and *amūrta* (in the statement of) what pertains to the body.[3] [68]

[1]This refers to BU statement: *athādhyātman* ....
[2]This is translation of *kīrtana*.
[3]This purports to be the beginning of the discussion of BU 2.3.4ff.

Now follows the discussion of BU 2.3.4-5 (from verse 68d) up to verse 82.

भूतत्रयं पृथिव्यादि देहेऽपि परिगृह्यते ।
मूर्तशब्देन यत्प्राणहृद्व्योम्नश्चापरं च यत् ॥६९॥

The triad of elements, beginning with earth is grasped even in a body, which is signified by the word *mūrta*, viz. that which is other than Prāṇa and the Sky (i.e. space)[1] in the heart. [69]

[1]We have ignored the reading of NKL edition *yat* in the place of *hṛd*.

चक्षूरसस्त्रयाणां स्याद्विशेषेणात्र निष्ठितम् ।
तेजः सर्वशरीरस्य निर्मातृ स्यादसंशयः ॥७०॥

Here,[1] the eye is the essence (or, cause) of the three (elements) wherein abides, without any doubt, fire which is the creator of whole body. [70]

This explains *etasya sataḥ*, (for already *etan martyam* etc. is explained).

SP and NKL cite the passage *ādityaś cakṣur bhūtvākṣiṇī prāviśat* (*Aitareyopaniṣad* 1.2.4) as the basis for this; cf. BU 1.3.3. There is thus *cakṣus* used as a synonym for *tejas*.

प्रथमा संस्कृतिरिति मन्त्रवर्णोऽपि दृश्यते ।
शश्वद्वै रेतस इति तथा च श्रुतिशासनम् ॥७१॥

Also there is noticed the Mantra *prathamā saṃskṛtiḥ* ....[1] So also there is instruction in the Śruti *śaśvad vai retasaḥ* ....[2] [71]

The verse cites a Śruti and a Brāhmaṇa in support of the statement in the preceding verse.

[1]Cf. *sā prathamā saṃskṛtir viśvavāra, sa prathamo varuṇo mitro 'gniḥ— Vājasaneyi Saṃhitā* (of Yajurveda) 7.14. In this, there is reference to *prathamasṛṣṭā dṛṣṭi*.

[2]Cf. *śaśvad vai retasaḥ siktasya cakṣuṣī prathame saṃbhavataḥ* (untraceable).

There now follows the view of Bhartṛprapañca which is to be accepted in this context.

मूर्तामर्तविभागोऽयं यदि नामेह भण्यते ।
अधिदैवं तथाध्यात्मं तथापीयान्न गृह्यते ॥७२॥

If, indeed, here (in the Śruti and Brāhmaṇa stated) this is stated as the division of what has a form and what does not have a form with reference to sphere of the deities and also to the sphere of the body, even then this is not to be taken to be this much.[1] [72]

SP points out how Sureśvara states in this verse that the view of Bhartṛprapañca regarding the division of *mūrta-amūrta* is not against the Śruti statements mentioned above.

[1]This division of *mūrta-amūrta* should not be taken as exhausted because it implies many more divisions within. This

invites the argument in the next verse.

कृत्स्नस्य ब्रह्मणो रूपे मूर्तामूर्ते विवक्षिते ।
यतोऽतो नेयता कात्स्न्र्यं देवताध्यात्मयोर्भवेत् ॥७३॥

Since it is intended to express the two forms of the entire Brahman,[1] viz. what has a form and what does not have a form; therefore, only by this much (description) there is not fullness of the description of the sphere of gods and that of body. [73]

[1]This refers to the entire creation caused (as it is supposed) by the Brahman.

आरब्धकार्यभूतानां गृहीतौ न च संभवः ।
यथोक्तलक्षणस्येह मुख्यवृत्त्योक्तभूमिषु ॥७४॥

There is no possibility of the given description to include, by (the) primary function (of its words) all the elements that have begun to produce their effects, among the various levels (of creation). [74]

This is one more reason that points out the insufficiency of the description.

व्याप्येव लक्षणं युक्तमन्यथा तदलक्षणम् ।
निर्देशस्तुपरिच्छिन्नविषयोऽत्राभिधीयते ॥७५॥

The definition should be all-pervasive;[1] if it is not so, it is not a definition and here the mention is made of what has only a limited sphere. [75]

The argument in this verse is: The division (i.e. definition) of the Brahman as *mūrta* and *amūrta* cannot—in its primary sense—be really applicable to all the five elements (which comprise the Brahman) and yet it should be applied to (all) the five elements. It is answered away in the second line; that is to say: *mūrta* and *amūrta* are used for only limited number of elements, viz. three and two.

[1]That is, it is applicable to all relevant items.

तत्रैवं सति यत्र स्यान्मूर्ताद्युक्तं चतुष्टयम् ।
लक्षणं तत्र संपूर्णमन्त्यकारणकार्ययोः ॥७६॥

This being so, that should be considered as full definition wherein there is stated the group of the four, viz. what has a form etc.[1] which is stated and all that falls between the two finals, viz. effects and their causes.[2] [76]

[1]Namely, *mūrta*, *martya* etc.

[2]Read SP: *apyayakramaṇāntye kāraṇe catuṣṭayāmūrtāmṛtādi tatrobhayatra lakṣaṇaṃ pūrṇamiti yathāyogaṃ lakṣyavyavahāra-siddhir ity arthaḥ.*

आकाशशब्दवाच्यो यः सर्वकारणकारणः ।
मुख्यवृत्त्या समर्थं स्यात्तत्रैवामूर्तलक्षणम् ॥७७॥

Only with reference to that the one, who is the cause of all causes, is to be expressed by the word *ākāśa*, the definition of what does not have a form will be suitable in its primary sense, only with reference to that. [77]

Verses 77-79 clarify the thought of verse 76 above. For profit, read NKL: *amūrtalakṣaṇam avyākṛtamātraviṣayaṃ mūrtalakṣaṇaṃ pṛthivīmātraviṣayam ityarthaḥ.*

पृथिव्यां चापि तन्मुख्यं यदुक्तं मूर्तलक्षणम् ।
उभयोरन्तरालस्था मिथः संकीर्णलक्षणाः ॥७८॥

And what is given as the definition of what has a form is principally signifying the earth and then there are other definitions intermixing with one another, which pertain to the different levels between the two (Sky and Earth). [78]

लक्षणं गौणमेव स्यादन्त्ययोर्मध्यभूमिषु ।
मूर्तामूर्तव्यवहृतिस्तथा तत्रापि दृश्यते ॥७९॥

Definition would be secondary in the case of the levels between the two finals; so also, there is noticed among them the use of the word signifying 'what has a form' and 'what does not have a form'. [79]

मुख्यवृत्तिग्रहायातो व्यापिलक्षणसिद्धये ।
क्षित्यादिवियदन्तं स्यान्मूर्तामूर्तस्य लक्षणम् ॥८०॥

Therefore, for accepting the primary function (of the words) and for achieving an all-pervasive definition, the definition of what has a form and what does not have a form should be what begins with the Earth and ends in the Sky. [80]

This is the end of Bhartṛprapañca's view.

योऽयं दक्षिणेऽक्षन्निति शास्त्रदृष्टत्वकारणात् ।
दक्षिणेऽक्षणि लिङ्गस्य विशेषः कश्चिदिष्यते ॥८१॥

[Now follows the purport of the specific statement *yo 'yaṃ dakṣiṇe akṣan ....*]

The Śruti statement 'This one who is noticed in the right eye' is made because it is seen by the scripture. Here is understood (lit. desired) some special aspect of the subtle (form of the Brahman). [81]

वीर्यवद्दक्षिणं लोकेऽप्यङ्गं दृष्टं यतस्ततः ।
दक्षिणेऽक्षन्निति वचः श्रुतेर्यत्नादिहेष्यते ॥८२॥

Since it is noticed in the world that the right part (of a body) is powerful, therefore, in this (context), the statement of the Śruti *dakṣiṇe 'kṣan* ... is accepted with purpose. [82]

Now follows the discussion of BU 2.3.6.

पिण्डप्राणविभागेन ह्यध्यात्मे चाधिदैवते ।
मूर्तामूर्तात्मनोरुक्तो विभागो ब्रह्मरूपयोः ॥८३॥

(Thus) by the division of the body and Prāṇa in relation to physical sphere and sphere of gods there is given division of the two forms of the Brahman which are having a form and not having a form. [83]

अथाधुना यथोक्तस्य तस्यैव करणात्मनः ।
लिङ्गस्य रूपं वक्ष्यामो वासनामयमात्मनः ॥८४॥

Now we shall state the form of the subtle form of the Ātman within, which is already mentioned and which is of the nature of impressions. [84]

मूर्तामूर्तादिसंबन्धाद्वासना लिङ्गमाश्रिताः ।
स्वाभासभ्रमदोषेण तन्मयः पुरुषो मतः ॥८५॥

Impressions have clung to the subtle form of the Brahman owing to their connection with what has a form and what does not have a form and owing to the fault consisting in the error of (seeing) the sentient being in its own appearance, it is taken to be full of them, i.e. the impression. [85]

अनेकवासनाचित्रं तल्लिङ्गं पटभित्तिवत् ।
मायेन्द्रजालसदृशं व्यामोहास्पदमात्मनः ॥८६॥
एतावन्मात्रमेवेति यत्र भ्रान्ता निरागमाः ।
विज्ञानवादिनो बौद्धास्तथा नैयायिकादयः ॥८७॥
आत्मनो द्रव्यभूतस्य यदेतद्वासनात्मकम् ।
रूपं गुणोऽस्य संसार इति वैशेषिकादयः ॥८८॥

That subtle form of the Ātman is variegated by numerous impressions like a picture-scroll on the wall; it is similar to a magic show and is subjected to delusion, [86]
and with reference to which the Bauddhas of the school of

Vijñānavāda who do not follow Vedas and also the Naiyāyikas, who (i.e. both of whom) are mistaken, hold this one [1] to be only this much [2] [87]
(and have understood) this Ātman, which is (already) a *dravya* 'matter' as having a form and properties, viz. its transmigratory existence, constituted by what is impression.[3] The Vaiśeṣikas (also are similarly mistaken). [88]

[1]Namely, the *liṅga* in verse 84 above.
[2]That is, *buddhimātram*, *ahaṃvṛttiviśiṣṭa*, *svarasabhaṅgura* and *rāgādikaluṣa* and not another that is *sthāyin*. In the case of the Bauddhas, they hold it to be momentary.
[3]SP: *tadīyabhrāntiṃ prakaṭayati* which NKL clarifies as *tārkikabhrānti*. This connects *vaiśeṣikādayaḥ* with *bhrāntāḥ*.

त्रिगुणं सत्प्रधानस्थं पुरुषार्थेन हेतुना ।
प्रवर्तते स्वतन्त्रं सदिदमित्यपि कापिलाः ॥८९॥

And Sāṃkhyas also [1] have said that this is but the independent existent (being) which proceeds to activity for the achieving of its end, resting on the Pradhāna made up of three *guṇas*. [89]

[1]Construe: *kāpilāḥ api*.

Sureśvara cites the view of Bhartṛprapañca whom he blames as 'not a true knower of Vedānta' in verses 96-104ab.

अप्यौपनिषदंमन्याः केचिदत्यन्तनैपुणात् ।
प्रक्रियां रचयित्वाहुर्वेदान्तार्थाविपश्चितः ॥९०॥

And also some thinkers,[1] who have really not known the nature of Vedānta and who have considered themselves as followers of the Upaniṣads,[2] have developed some kind of system with great skill! [90]

[1]This is a mockingly regardful description of, or with reference

to Bhartṛprapañca.

[2]That is, the words which constitute the so-called theory of Vedānta.

यावान्बाह्यो विकारः स्यात्क्षेत्रज्ञपरिवेष्टनः ।
अध्यात्मं चाधिदैवं वा नामरूपविभागतः ॥९१॥
अव्याकृताद्व्याकृतः स्यादेतावानेव सोऽत्र तु ।
मूर्तो वा यदि वामूर्तः सच्च त्यच्चेति भण्यते ॥९२॥

Whatever be the external modification is[1] all here, whether having a form or not having a form, is called *sat* and also *tyat* and that one which is wrapped by the self within (lit. the knower of the field) whether in relation to the body or to the sphere of deities, and divided into name and form and which has become as the modified from the unmodified, is here[2] only this much. [91-92]

This explains the *prakriyā* mentioned in the preceding verse.

[1]*syāt = asti*.

[2]That is, *etāvān* referring to the Ātman described earlier as *mūrta*, *amūrta*, *sat* and *tyat*.

प्राणानामपि सत्यत्वं भूतसत्याभिसंगतेः ।
कथं यतस्त्वमी सर्वे प्राणाः क्षेत्रज्ञलक्षणाः ॥९३॥
अनामरूपकाः सन्तः सत्यसंयोगहेतुतः ।
देहिनः प्राणवत्साक्षात्संवृत्ता नामरूपिणः ॥९४॥
निर्देशाय च कल्पन्ते प्राणा वा इति नान्यथा ।
तदत्र निखिलं सत्यं श्रुत्या संशोधितं स्फुटम् ॥९५॥

*prāṇa*s are also described as being the *satya* 'truth', because they are associated with the elements that are the *satya*. (Someone asks:) How? (The answer is:) Since the *prāṇa*s are modifications (or adjuncts) of the knower of the field and, having no name and form, they exist on account of their connection with the truth (viz. the organs) as the organs of the embodied and they become perceptible (and come to) have name and form and become fit for the description that they are now *prāṇa*s (and are) not otherwise and all this is the whole truth, clearly presented to us by the Śruti. [93-94-95]

This is Bhartṛprapañca's explanation of *prāṇa vai satyam* ... *satyāya satyam*. The first *satya* refers to the elements which later on become the second *satya*, viz. *prāṇa*s 'organs'. Thus, this is the explanation of what appears as creation and which is different organs of a human body. This is a kind of system that Bhartṛprapañca suggested.

व्याविद्धसत्यराशेः स्याद्विज्ञानात्मन एव तु ।
स्वरूपं यत्तदधुना वक्तव्यमवशिष्यते ॥९६॥

But that nature of the inner self which has thus appeared[1] from the entire mass of truth is now left to be explained now. [96]

Verses 93-95 have described the modifications of Vijñānātman and in what follows in verses 97-99 is the description of Vijñānātman.

[1] *vyāviddha* = *vyākṛta* of verse 92 above.

तत्रैतस्यामवस्थायां विभागो विनिवर्तते ।
अयं भोक्ता विज्ञानात्मा तथा दैवतिकास्त्वमी ॥९७॥
विज्ञानात्मान इत्येष भेदहेतुनिवर्तनात् ।
यत आधारगो ह्येष नामरूपादिलक्षणः ॥९८॥
विशेषो न स्वतस्तच्च नामरूपादि शोधितम् ।
संशोध्य तदिदं सर्वं विज्ञानात्मा प्रदर्श्यते ॥९९॥

There, i.e. in this state of Vijñānātman, any division[1] ceases to exist; namely, this one is the enjoyer and this one is the inner self and these are (different) deities. [97]
Since the cause of (any) difference is set aside by the word *vijñānātmānaḥ*, since this specification depends on some basis

which has a form and name and form, it does not exist on its own account, therefore that name; and the form (of any modification) was explained (by the Śruti)—therefore, thus having described all that (only) as Vijñānātman is shown.[98-99]

In verses 93-95 the division meant the enjoyer of the means to enjoyment and also different deities related to them; thus the division does not differ there.
Sureśvara uses *daivatikāḥ* for *devatāḥ*.
[1]Namely, different organs, *vibhāga*.

सर्वेषामपि तेनेदं समानं लक्षणं भवेत् ।
क्षेत्रज्ञानां विशेषोऽत्र यतो नैवोपपद्यते ॥१००॥

Therefore, this is the description of all the knowers of the field, for the reason that there does not appear to be any (reasonable) distinction between one and another of them. [100]

Here, Bhartṛprapañca appears to consider, like the Sāṃkhyas, that there are many Puruṣas that are similar to one another.

एतस्य पुरुषस्येति रूपं निर्दिश्यतेऽधुना ।
पुंसो रूपमुपक्षीणं मूर्तामूर्तसमाश्रयम् ॥१०१॥

And now is described in the words *etasya puruṣasya* the form of the Puruṣa, since all that, which pertains to (lit. depends on) what has a form and what does not have a form is so far fully explained (lit. exhaustively stated). [101]

This is the explanation of *tasya haitasya puruṣasya vijñānātmano rūpaṃ nirdiśyate*.

येन त्वस्य विशेषेण विज्ञानात्मत्वमिष्यते ।
विभज्यमानस्य सतः परस्मादात्मनोऽद्वयात् ॥१०२॥
अपाञ्चभौतिकं रूपमिह तन्निर्दिदिक्ष्यते ।
यथेति माहारजनं वासनोपचयात्मकम् ॥१०३॥

तस्य हैतस्य संबन्धमेवं केचित्प्रचक्षते ।

Here is now sought to point out that the form of the Ātman, which is not comprising five elements (and) whereby, i.e. by what specification is understood the nature of it as the inner self, i.e. being distinguished from the highest self which is without (any) duality. In the words *yathā māhārajanam* ... that is (described as) comprised of mass of impressions.[1] [102-103]
Thus do some explain the relation of the statement *tasya haitasya* (with *yathā māhārajanam* ...) [104ab]

[1]The earlier parts of these verses (viz. 101ff.) clarify *samānaṃ lakṣaṇaṃ kṣetrajñānām* in the preceding verse (i.e. verse 100). The last quarter of verse 103 refers to the passage in BU which Bhartṛprapañca holds as the proper introduction of the description of Vijñānātman.

In verses 104-111, Sureśvara discusses the wrong in Bhartṛprapañca's view on the connection of tasya ha ... which is mentioned in verse 103.

तदयुक्तं यथान्यायस्तथायमभिधीयते ॥१०४॥

(But) that is not proper, since it is an improper explanation. (How this is) we shall now say (in the following). [104cd]

This is Sureśvara's remark of the non-acceptance of the view which is stated so far.

पुष्पादिवासनानां हि वस्त्रादिष्वेव संगतिः ।
सजातीयेषु नियता दृश्यते नान्यजातिषु ॥१०५॥

In the case of fragrances (lit. impressions) of flowers etc. they necessarily continue to be resting only in the garment etc. which are similar in kind and they are not seen in those which belong to other (kinds). [105]

This is to state *ātmā na vāsanāśrayaḥ*. In the first line, Sureśvara refers to flowers and similar things (*dravyas*), which means some specific things. These are in contrast with individual selves (not *dravyas*) that are not of the kind of flowers (*sajātīya*) and therefore the argument about the impressions, which is adduced, cannot apply to the subtle inner self. Cf. verses 117-118 below.

द्रव्येऽपि न खलु व्योम्नि वासना काचिदीक्ष्यते ।
अद्रव्ये चासजातीये चैतन्ये वासना कुतः ॥१०६॥

Though sky is a *dravya*,[1] there is not noticed any impression on it; therefore, how can there be impressions on sentience which is not *dravya*, and which is not of the same kind (of a flower etc.)? [106]

The argument in verse 105 is clarified here further even in the case of the sky which is not of the same kind (*vijātīya*) as the flower there is not any impression noticed therefore the second line follows by *kaumutikanyāya*.

[1]So in Nyāya terminology.

वासनाकारतां गच्छेच्चैतन्यं चेत्कपालवत् ।
वासनानिष्फलत्वं स्याच्चैतन्यादपृथक्स्थितेः ॥१०७॥

If it is held that sentience (*jīva*) assume the form of impression(s), it would be like a potsherd;[1] therefore, since sentience remains apart from them (viz. various parts of a body), there would not be any result produced by impressions. [107]

This sets aside the notion that impressions (*vāsanās*) are non-distinct from the Ātman.

[1]That is, perishable, or, liable to destruction.

न हि श्रोत्रोत्थविज्ञानं रूपवासनयाञ्ज्यते ।
विषयत्वाविशेषेऽपि कुतोऽसङ्गत्वतश्चितेः ॥१०८॥

Indeed, knowledge that arises from ears (etc.) cannot be marked[1] by impressions of the form, even if the two[2] are not distinct, objects of perception that they are; how then can sentience (be by marked impressions) since it has no contact with any organs? [108]

This is for setting aside an alternative notion that impressions are distinct from the Ātman.

[1]NKL reads *añcyate* for *añjyate*.

[2]Namely, knowledge mentioned and impressions.

षड्भावविक्रियाणां च निषेधश्चेतनात्मनः ।
असङ्ग इति चाप्युक्तिरसकृच्छ्रूयते श्रुतौ ॥१०९॥

Also, there is denial, in the case of the sentient Ātman, of the six modifications of becomings (objects);[1] for the statement (about the Ātman that) it is not having a contact (with any other thing) is several times heard. [109]

Thus blame is given to Bhartṛprapañca that his theorization is opposed to the Śruti. It states that sentience is immutable (*kūṭastha*) and it cannot be in contact with impressions.

[1]These refer to the six modifications stated in *Nirukta* 1.2.

भूतसंयोगतः प्राप्तं न च तत्पाञ्चभौतिकम् ।
इति ब्रुवाणो लोकेऽस्मिन्हस्यते बालकैरपि ॥११०॥

In this world, one who postulates that (a thing) is obtained from conjunction of elements and it is still not made up of those five elements, is scoffed at even by children. [110]

मर्तामूर्तविभागेऽस्य विभागो विनिवर्तते ।
इति स्वोक्तमविस्मृत्य वासनाभेदगीः कथम् ॥१११॥

How can there be the statement about the variety of impressions by one who has forgotten his own statement,[1] viz. that there does not remain any division in the case of this one, even if division of it into what has a form and what does not have a form (has been already made by the Śruti)? [111]

This is to blame Bhartṛprapañca for the fault of self-contradiction. This is noticeable from verse 87 above which accepts the *bhoktṛ-bhogya* division. The argument thus pertains to the *bhoktṛ-bhogya* relation consequent upon *mūrta-amūrta* division of the Brahman—here, Jīva is meant.

In verses 112-124, Sureśvara gives an exposition of Bhartṛ-prapañca's view on the prakriyā mentioned in verse 90 above.

रचयन्ति तथासाध्वीं प्रक्रियां न्यायवर्जिताम् ।
मूर्तामूर्तात्मको राशिरेको बाह्यः किलेष्यते ॥११२॥
उत्तमः परमात्माख्यो राशिरत्राभिधीयते ।
मध्यमोऽयं तृतीयस्तु ताभ्यां राशिः प्रयोजकः ॥११३॥

Thus, (the scholars)[1] develop into a proper system which is devoid of reasoning: They[1] accept that there is one mass consisting in what has a form and what does not have a form; (this is) accepted (as lying) outside (the teaching of Śruti) [112]
and there is then stated (in their theory) a second[2] mass called the highest Ātman; and this third one apart from them, called Madhyama is proposed by them as causing[3] the two (masses). [113]

[1]This refers to Bhartṛprapañca in plural, which is out of mock respect.
[2]This is for *uttama*.
[3]Cf. NKL: *prayojakaḥ utpādakaḥ mūrtāmūrtarāśeḥ*.

पाणिपेषोत्थितेनायं कर्त्रा भोक्त्रा सहात्मना ।

भावनाज्ञानकर्मादिसमुदायः प्रयोजकः ॥११४॥
मूर्तामूर्तादिराशिस्तु प्रयोज्यः साधनं तथा ।
तार्किकैः सह संधिं च चिकीर्षन्ति यथाबलम् ॥११५॥

This one (viz. the Madhyama) is the cause (lit. producer), together with the agent, the enjoyer, viz. the Ātman who has risen (from sleep) due to the shaking by hand, a mass of impressions, knowledge, activity etc.[1] [114]
The (entire) mass of what has a form and what does not have a form etc.[2] is to be set to activity (*prayojya*) and also the means of activity; and they[3] make an agreement with the logicians according to their capacity (strength of mind). [115]

Cf. SP citing (possibly Bhartṛprapañca's statement): *sa eṣa vidyākarma pūrvaprajñārūpo 'sya karmaṇo bāhyaṃ mūrtāmūrtaṃ sādhanaṃ yad upādāya kāryakaraṇavato bhogasiddhir iti rāśi-trayaṃ kalpayitvā kalpanāntaram api kurvantīti.* For clarification of Sureśvara's cryptic explanation, refer to BUB: *kartrā bhoktrā vijñānamayenājātaśatrupratibodhitena saha vidyākarmapūrvaprajñā-samudāyaḥ prayoktā karmarāśiḥ prayojyaḥ pūrvokto mūrtāmūrta-bhūtarāśiḥ sādhanaṃ ceti.*
[1]The word etc. refers to attachment (and other feelings (?)).
[2]The word etc. refers to *martya*, *amṛta*, *sthita*, *sat* and *tyat*.
[3]Referring to Bhartṛprapañca.

अयं प्रयोजको राशिर्लिङ्गमेव किलाश्रितः ।
इत्युक्त्वा सांख्यत्वभयात्कल्पयन्ति ततोऽन्यथा ॥११६॥

This mass, which causes the (i.e. sets to) activity (the other mass, viz.) the *liṅga* has resorted to the subtle form (of Hiraṇyagarbha) and thus then they are a little apprehensive of being called as Sāṃkhyas and therefore explain (the idea) in yet another way. [116]

The argument is: The statement *karmarāśir liṅgāśritaḥ* would mean acceptance of the Sāṃkhya view. Therefore, the exponent of the view explains his opinion in the following verses, in the way the logicians do.

गन्धः पुष्पाश्रयो यद्वत्पुटमाश्रित्य तिष्ठति ।
कुसुमापागमेऽप्येवं लिङ्गस्था वासनात्मनि ॥११७॥

As fragrance residing in a flower remains after resorting to its wrapper[1] even after the flower has disappeared, in the same way, impression which resides in the subtle form (viz. *liṅga*) stays in the Ātman. [117]

Cf. verse 105 above. Read a note by the editor of the NKL edition: *liṅgāśritā vāsanā ātmānam āśrayate puṣpāśrito gandhaḥ puṣpaviyoge 'pi puṭatailam iva. liṅgād āgatena saguṇo bhavati paramātmaikadeśaḥ svato nirguṇo 'pi. sa vijñānātmā badhyate mucyate ca iti kalpanayā tārkikasaṃvādam api kurvanti iti samudāyabhāvaḥ*. This explains *anyathā kalpayanti*.

[1]Cf. note 1 on verse 159 below.

वासनाकामकर्माणि लिङ्गस्थान्येव नात्मनि ।
लिङ्गादात्मानमायान्ति गन्धो गन्धपुटं यथा ॥११८॥

Impression, desire and activity are all residing in the subtle form (of the Vijñānātman) and not in sentience proper; they come to the Ātman from the subtle form in the same way as the fragrance (of the flowers) to what has wrapped the fragrance, i.e. the flower. [118]

This is amplification of verse 117.

निर्गुणोऽपि परैकांशो बहिरभ्यागतेन सः ।
कर्मणा सगुणः साक्षाद्भवतीति प्रचक्षते ॥११९॥
ततश्च कर्ता भोक्ता च बध्यते मुच्यते तथा ।
विज्ञानात्मेति कणभुक्चित्तमेवं समाश्रिताः ॥१२०॥

Then this portion of the highest self, though it does not have any properties, seems to be possessed of properties by the external adventitious activity—thus do they explain. [119]

And from that it (viz. the Vijñānātman) becomes the agent (of the activity) and the enjoyer (of the result), it gets bound and becomes released. Thus have they taken recourse to the thought of Kaṇāḍa. [120]

भतराशेरगाल्लिङ्गं कर्मराशिः सकाशतः ।
लिङ्गादात्मानमागात्स लिङ्गसंबन्धकारणात् ॥१२१॥
कृष्णशक्तिरविद्यापि परस्मादेव सोत्थिता ।
विकृत्य परमात्मांशं विज्ञानात्मनि तिष्ठति ॥१२२॥

The entire mass of activity has come from the mass of elements and then owing to its association[1] with the subtle (of the Vijñānātman) it has proceeded from the subtle form to the Ātman (i.e. sentience). [121]

The power of (Lord) Kṛṣṇa which is but ignorance (i.e. which has in reality) arisen from highest (Ātman) and, modifying the portion of the highest Ātman, it remains there in the individual self. [122]

It appears that Sureśvara is feeling the thought of Vaiṣṇava and seeks to explain it in the same way as the logicians.

[1]It literally means nearness, a kind of *tadātmya* as it were.

यथोषरात्मको दोषः पृथिव्या एव जज्ञिवान् ।
क्ष्मैकदेशं विकृत्यास्तेऽविद्या तद्वत्परात्मनः ॥१२३॥

As one has known that the barren land which is but a defect of the (entire) earth, has affected only a part of the earth; so also ignorance (affects only a portion) of the highest self. [123]

This explains how *avidyā* affects only a Jīva which is but a part of the highest Ātman, even if it (viz. *avidyā*) rises from it (i.e. Ātman). The view of the Sāṃkhyas is understood from Bhartṛprapañca's holding *karmarāśi* as *antaḥkaraṇadharma* and *avidyā* as *anātmadharma*.

अनात्मधर्मोऽविद्येति वदन्तश्चोषरादिवत् ।
इत्येवं सांख्यसिद्धान्तमनुवर्तन्ति संभ्रमात् ॥१२४॥

Thus, saying that ignorance is a property of the non-Ātman, like a barren land etc. (of the entire earth), they are really following[1] the doctrine of the Sāṃkhyas, owing to some confusion.[2] [124]

Sureśvara points out that Bhartṛprapañca, though he follows the way of Naiyāyikas' argument, follows in reality the Sāṃkhyas.

[1]*anuvartanti* is in Vedic style for *anuvartante*.

[2]That he follows the doctrine of the Sāṃkhyas results only from confusion, for it is already stated that Bhartṛprapañca has chosen to follow the logicians.

In verses 125-137, Sureśvara controverts Bhartṛprapañca's notion of the prakriyā running through verses 112-124.

नैवं कल्पयितुं युक्तं वेदसिद्धान्तबाधनात् ।
पुरापि चैतदुदितं यथा वेदान्तबाधनम् ॥१२५॥

It is not proper to think like this, because it involves contradiction with the established doctrine of the Veda; and as to contradiction to the Vedānta, we have said earlier.[1] [125]

[1]NKL calls it *vṛddhavicāra* and SP, *bṛhadvicāra*, which is the same as the thought expressed in the SV 181ab-184.

सकलत्वे परस्योक्ताः संसारित्वादिलक्षणाः ।
दोषाः सर्वेऽपि चायान्ति प्रत्यगात्मानमेकलम् ॥१२६॥

By the acceptance of the highest self as comprising the whole (world), there come to be attached to the inner self which is just alone, all the faults characterized as being transmigratory etc. [126]

This clarifies the idea in verse 125cd above.

क्षेत्रज्ञस्य च संभित्तौ परस्मादात्मनः स्वतः ।
एकत्वसंभवोऽत्यन्तं क्षेत्रज्ञपरमात्मनोः ॥१२७॥

If the knower of the field is taken to be different from highest Ātman, then there follows of itself the utter impossibility of the uniqueness of the highest self and of the knower of the field. [127]

This thus leads to opposition to Śruti; refer to the well-known Mahāvākya *tat tvaṁ asi*.

अथोपचारतो देशो लिङ्गमेवात्मनो मतः ।
न तदा लिङ्गविध्वस्तौ वासनात्मनि युज्यते ॥१२८॥

If (however) one understands by metaphor that the subtle form (of the Vijñānātman) is the part of the Ātman, then there would not remain (any) impression in the Ātman, when the subtle form (of the Vijñānātman) is destroyed. [128]

This argument proceeds from a possible supposition that the *liṅga* is a part of the Ātman itself. The supposition can be answered away in the following statement: *liṅgābhāve 'pi liṅgasthā vāsanā jīve tiṣṭhati iti svaśāstrāsiddhiḥ*.

न्यायः पुरोदितो योऽत्र वासनासंश्रयं प्रति ।
स सर्वोऽत्रानुसंधेयः पूर्वपक्षापनुत्तये ॥१२९॥

And the reason [1] stated before as regards the (Ātman) being related to impression has to be remembered fully (here) for the refutation of the *prima facie* view. [129]

This sets aside the notion that *vāsanā* rests in the Ātman.

[1]Refer to verses 106 and 117 above.

उत्थानं चाप्यविद्यायाः परस्मादात्मनः स्वतः ।
ऊषरादिवदित्यादिकल्पना नोपपद्यते ॥१३०॥

So also the notion about the rise of ignorance from the highest Ātman itself like the notion of (the earth being affected by) a barren land cannot stand to reason. [130]

अनिर्मोक्षप्रसक्तिः स्याद्यद्यविद्या परात्मनः ।
निरात्मवादसक्तिश्च मोहोच्छेदे भवेदिह ॥१३१॥

Further, there would result absence of liberation, if (it is posited that) ignorance belongs to the highest Ātman and, when infatuation is removed, there would only result the theory that there is no Ātman. [131]

This points to undesirable results which arise from accepting *avidyā* to rest in the highest Ātman.

वास्यदेशातिरेकेण वासनाया न चेष्यते ।
देशान्तरोपगमनं गुणवद्द्रव्यवर्जनात् ॥१३२॥

It is not accepted that an impression shifts from one region to another which is different from where that (impression) existed (earlier) even like a property (moving to another substance) after leaving one substance. [132]

A property of a thing is innate in it; it does not leave that thing and go to another. Similarly an impression does not leave one abode and move to another. This argument was evoked by the illustration of fragrance of a flower stated earlier.[1]

[1] Cf. verse 118 above.

सामञ्जस्येन गच्छन्ति न च श्रुत्यक्षराण्यपि ।
यथोक्तकल्पनायां हि न युक्ता तेन कल्पना ॥१३३॥

Since (*hi*) by accepting the theory (of Bhartṛprapañca) stated earlier, the statements[1] in the Śruti also do not get properly understood;[2] therefore, that theory is not reasonable. [133]

This is one more reason for holding that *vāsanā* cannot have a support in the Ātman. In this and the next two verses, a reference is made to Śaṅkara that was opposed.

[1]It literally means: letters.

[2]That is, 'they do not go well with reason'.

कामः संकल्प इत्याद्या मनसो धर्मिणः श्रिताः ।
धर्मा न त्वात्मनः शास्त्रे ह्यसङ्गो हीति वारणात् ॥१३४॥

Desire, resolution etc. are properties heard in the scriptures as belonging to *manas* which has (those) properties and not of the Ātman, because in the scriptural text *asaṅgo hi* ...[1] there is clear denial (of any property). [134]

Cf. BU 1.5.2 for *kāmasaṃkalpa*.

The words *manas*, *hṛdaya* in the following verse are used for the Ātman. NKL: *uktaśrutigatamanohṛdayādiśabdānām ātmavacanatvāt* (note on NKL:) *ātmā ucyate anena iti vyutpattyā ātmabodhanatvād ity arthaḥ*.

[1]Cf. BU 4.3.15: *asaṅgo hy ayaṃ puruṣa iti*.

हृदये ह्येव रूपाणि ध्यायतीवेति चापरम् ।
कामा येऽस्य हृदीत्यादि तीर्णो हीति तथा वचः ॥१३५॥

'Only in the heart does he ponder over, as it were, the forms' is another (statement), so also is there the sentence 'He has indeed crossed over those desires which are in his heart'. [135]

श्रुतादर्थान्न चान्योऽर्थो यथोक्तवचसां यतः ।
सम्यक्कल्पयितुं शक्यः कल्पनातो न युज्यते ॥१३६॥

Since it is not possible to consider the meaning of the sentences quoted above as other than what can be the meaning heard from Śruti; therefore, the theory (of Bhartṛprapañca) is not reasonable. [136]

प्रत्यग्ब्रह्मत्वसिद्ध्यर्था सर्वैवोपनिषत्त्वियम् ।
तावन्मात्रपरत्वेन वेदान्तानामुपक्षयात् ॥१३७॥

And in fact this entire Upaniṣad is for establishing that the inner self is but the Brahman; therefore, all the Vedas do culminate in only that much as the instrument. [137]

In other words, the Vedas do not say any more than the *pratyagbrahmatva*.

There follows now the refutation of three different masses proposed by Bhartṛprapañca.

राशित्रितयपक्षे च नाप्यर्थोऽत्र समञ्जसः ।
क्रियते कल्पना येन सर्वन्यायविरोधिनी ॥१३८॥

And also the meaning (of the Śruti) is not reasonably understood (*samañjasa*), if the theory of three groups (*rāśi*s) is accepted, (for) thereby[1] is accepted a notion which is opposed to all reason. [138]

[1]That is, in that theory, viz. the word *vāva*.

द्वे एव तु यदा रूपे मूर्तामूर्ते सवासने ।
ब्रह्म रूपि तृतीयं च तदा वावेति युज्यते ॥१३९॥
ब्रह्मैकदेशभूतस्य विज्ञानात्मन एव ते ।
रूपे इति तदा युक्तं कल्पनानुगुणं वचः ॥१४०॥

If it were that there were only two forms, having a form, and not having a form together with the impressions and, therefore, the Brahman were the third, viz. as having the two forms, only then the word *vāva* (in BU) would be reasonable. [139]

And when it held that the two forms[1] belong to the Vijñānātman which has been only included in the Brahman, only then the statement 'the Brahman has only two forms' would be in conformity with the theory. [140]

[1]Cf. verse 126 above.

विज्ञानात्ममुखेनाथ यदि वा परमात्मनः ।
रूपे इति तदावक्ष्यच्छ्रौती चेत्कल्पना भवेत् ॥१४१॥

Or, if the two forms [1] were to be of the highest Ātman through (their being the forms of) Vijñānātman, then one could have said that the theory is enunciated by the Śruti. [141]

Hereby Sureśvara suggests that this is not so stated by Śruti.
[1]Namely, *mūrta* and *amūrta*.

द्विवचश्च तथायुक्तं त्रैरूप्यस्येह संभवात् ।
मूर्तामूर्ते च द्वे रूपे तृतीयं वासना यतः ॥१४२॥

And thus statement of the two (forms) would have become unreasonable, since here (in the Śruti) there could be (contingent) the existence of three forms: thus, the two forms, viz. what has a form and what does not have a form, and the third (i.e.) impression. [142]

The argument is: The word *vāva* for specification (*avadhāraṇa*) would then be improper or unreasonable.

मतं मूर्तेतरे रूपे ब्रह्मणोऽभिमते सदा ।
क्षेत्रज्ञस्य तु नैवैते वासनामात्ररूपितः ॥१४३॥
तदापि जीवद्वारेण विक्रियां व्रजतो विभोः ।
वासनाद्यभिसंबन्ध इतीयं गीरनर्थिका ॥१४४॥

It may be held that the two forms *mūrta* and the other (i.e. *amūrta*) are of the Brahman and not of that knower of the field, since it is only of the nature of impression(s).[1] [143]
(But) in that case also, the all-pervasive would be undergoing

modification through the individual self and, therefore, the statement that it is connected with impression would be meaningless. [144]

The argument in verse 143 proceeds from the acceptance of *vāsanā* as the form/nature of Jīva (i.e. *jīvarūpa*). And that in verse 144 proceeds from the contingency of *vāsanā*s being related to the Brahman through a Jīva thus disproving *mūrta* and *amūrta* as being two forms of what undergoes modification, viz. Jīva. [1]The word *vāsanāmātrarūpitaḥ* is for *-rūpitvataḥ*.

वासनानामपि यतो न विशेषो मनागपि ।
क्षेत्रज्ञद्वारतायाः स्यादसत्तस्माद्विकल्पितम् ॥१४५॥

This is so because even impressions do not even slightly differ (from *mūrta* and *amūrta*); therefore this notion (about) impressions through their relation to the knower of the field is wrongly conceived. [145]

This adduces the reason for the argument in the preceding verse.

वस्तु वस्त्वन्तरत्वेन न च विक्रियतेऽञ्जसा ।
वृत्त्येह मुख्ययेत्येवं शक्यो वक्तुं जगत्यपि ॥१४६॥

And it does not smoothly follow that in this world one thing gets modified through (the modification of) another; it is not possible to state so in the primary meaning of the words. [146]

This argument is against the notion that Jīva is distinct from the highest Brahman.

वस्त्वन्तरं न च मतः क्षेत्रज्ञः परमात्मनः ।
सिद्धान्तहानिरेवं च कल्पनायां ध्रुवं भवेत् ॥१४७॥

And the knower of the field is not accepted as a thing different from the highest Ātman. Therefore, there is thus in this theory (of Bhartṛprapañca) the discarding of the doctrine of Vedānta. [147]

This argument is based on the acceptance of Jīva as not different from the Brahman.

आविश्चिकीर्षुभिस्तस्माद्वेदान्तार्थं महात्मभिः ।
ईदृशी कल्पनायुक्ता कृतं परहितार्थिभिः ॥१४८॥

Therefore it is unreasonable to hold the theory on the part of those who desire to clarify the meaning of Vedas and thereby achieve the well-being of others. [148]

This is concluding that Jīva serves as the substratum for *karma* etc. and that there can be postulated three masses.

Now follows the explanation of the word tat in tasya haitasya which is accepted by Sureśvara.

दक्षिणेऽक्षन्पुमानिति लिङ्गात्मा परिगृह्यते ।
अध्यात्मेऽथाधिदैवे च तस्यैव प्रकृतत्वतः ॥१४९॥

In the words (of the Śruti) *dakṣiṇe akṣan* ... it is the subtle form (of the Ātman), viz. the man, that is understood with reference to the body and also to the sphere of deities, because that itself is under reference.[1] [149]

[1]Cf. *ya eṣa* ... in this context.

जीवग्रहोऽत्र नन्वस्तु प्रकृतत्वाविशेषतः ।
तस्यैवैतानि रूपाणि कस्मान्नेत्यभिधीयताम् ॥१५०॥

(One might argue:) Let there be here accepted (a reference to) the individual self, since in the matter of being relevant it is not different;[1] then why could it not be said that these[2] are but its[3] forms? [150]

[1]That is, it is also under reference.
[2]This refers to impressions.
[3]That is, of the individual self.

नैवंरूपितया यस्मादिह श्रुत्या विवक्षितः ।
क्षेत्रज्ञः करणात्मैव तस्मादिह विवक्षितः ॥१५१॥

(The answer is:) This is not so, since the knower of the field is not here intended by the Śruti as having this nature;[1] therefore, here is intended only (that knower of the field) who has the nature of the deities. [151]

In verse 150 Jīva refers to the Vijñānātman possessing impressions and in verse 151 Kṣetrajña is understood as not tainted by any impressions, that is to say, it is not different from the Brahman.

[1]That is, having *vāsanā*s as it nature.

वासनानुगतं लिङ्गं मृद्वन्मृद्विक्रियात्मसु ।
चेत्यते साक्षिणा यस्मान्नातः क्षेत्रज्ञरूपिता ॥१५२॥

Since the subtle form (=Jīva), associated with impressions is revealed by the seer (=Kṣetrajña) just as clay is revealed in what are various modifications of clay, therefore (Jīva) does not have the character of Kṣetrajña. [152]

This explains why the Jīva (which is really not different from the Ātman) does not have the nature of being affected/characterized by *vāsanā*s. And it is argued that they belong to what is *citta*, a false 'modification' of the Brahman.

माहारजनमित्यादि रूपं चेत्साक्षिणो भवेत् ।
नेति नेतीत्यथादेशं नाकरिष्यत्तदात्मनः ॥१५३॥

If in the words *māhārajanam* ... there was intended the expression of the form of the seer,[1] Śruti would not have given the instruction (about the Brahman) in the words *neti neti*. [153]

Here is suggested that opposition of the Śruti to the objector's argument.

[1]That is, the Ātman.

अन्यस्यासौ न चादेशः शक्यो वक्तुं प्रमाणतः ।
नेति नेतीति तस्यैव षष्ठान्त उपसंहृतेः ॥१५४॥

And that instruction *neti neti* could not have been expressed with reference to another[1] in an authoritative way further, in the end of the sixth chapter[2] since the conclusion there is only in reference to that itself (viz. the seer).[3] [154]

[1]That is, other than the seer.

[2]The sixth, the traditional counting of chapters, means the fourth chapter. Refer to BU 4.4.22.

[3]The word in fourth chapter is the Ātman.

व्येव त्वेति प्रतिज्ञाया अर्थवत्त्वं तथा भवेत् ।
पाणिपेषोत्थितस्यैव यद्यादेशो भवेदयम् ॥१५५॥
पाणिपेषोत्थितोऽन्यश्चेन्नेतीति च ततोऽपरः ।
अन्योऽसाविति मिथ्या धीस्तदा स्यान्मोहकारणात् ॥१५६॥

Only in that way there will be meaningfulness of the enunciation *vy eva tvā*[1] .... If this instruction were of the one who is awakened by shaking by the hand, [155]
and, as a result, if that one, viz. awakened by shaking by the hand, were not different from that other than that then there would arise false knowledge owing to delusion. [156]

This is to assert that *neti neti* ... is the instruction about the inner self only (verse 155) and the same is asserted again (in verse 156) by way of *vyatireka*.

[1]Refer to BU 2.1.15.

न स्यादात्मानमेवावेदहं ब्रह्मेतिमानजा ।
सम्यग्धीर्निखिलध्वान्तघातिनी मुक्तिदायिनी ॥१५७॥

Further (i.e. in that case), there would not arise the right knowledge from an authoritative means (i.e. the Śruti statement *neti neti*), (the awareness:) I have known the Ātman, (and) I am Brahman, which destroys the entire darkness (i.e. ignorance) and effects liberation. [157]

This is to point out yet another fault in Bhartṛprapañca's theory.

करणात्मन एवातस्तस्य हेति ग्रहो भवेत् ।
न तु तत्साक्षिणो युक्तस्तस्य रूपनिषेधतः ॥१५८॥

Therefore, there can be in the words *tasya ha* the mention only of that *kāraṇātman*.[1] And it is not proper to be that of the seer, since there is denial of (any) form[2] of that. [158]

Cf. verse 151 above.
[1]This refers to *citta*, as noted under verse 152 above.
[2]That is, a body and its organs which come to have some knowledge.

वासना भूरिरूपास्ता लिङ्गस्था लिङ्गसाक्षिणः ।
कुर्वन्ति बहुरूपत्वं मणेरास्तरणं यथा ॥१५९॥

Impressions have many forms and, residing in the subtle form, they effect the multi-formed character of the seer in the subtle form, in the same way as a wrapper[1] (causes the appearance of varied forms) of a jewel. [159]

Here is stated how the appearance (*ābhāsa*) in the Jīva is caused through misapprehension (or, wrong understanding).
[1]Cf. NKL: *āstaraṇaṃ raktavastrādikam*.

माहारजनमित्यत्र हारिद्रं रूपमुच्यते ।
इन्द्रगोपोपमानेन कौसुम्भस्य गतत्वतः ॥१६०॥

In the word *māhārajana*, there is expressed the form of what is painted with turmeric, since, by the (use of) the standard of comparison, viz. Indragopa, the red colour is already conveyed. [160]

Verses 160-170 is Sureśvara's explanation, following Śaṅkara, of the meaning of BU 2.3.6.

SP seems to quote from Bhartṛprapañca: *uktam hi syāt kusumbhaṃ vahniśikhaṃ māhārajanam ity api iti*. But NKL cites the same quotation with the concluding remark *iti nāmaśāsanāt*.

पीतं वस्त्रं यथा तद्वल्लिङ्गमाभाति साक्षिणः ।
आस्त्र्यादिविषयोद्भूतवासनावासितं दृशेः ॥१६१॥

As there is yellow garment, so does there appear the subtle form of the seer, tainted (in the colour); it (viz. the seer) is affected by impressions rising from (various) objects (of enjoyment), viz. beginning with a woman etc. [161]

ईषत्पाण्डु यथोर्णादि तद्वल्लिङ्गं प्रकाशते ।
इन्द्रगोपोऽतिरक्तश्च भृशं रक्तं मनस्तथा ॥१६२॥

As a piece of wool etc.[1] appears slightly white, so does the subtle form appear (slightly white); and (as) an Indragopa appears extremely red; so is *manas* very much tainted by impressions. [162]

This explains *yathā pāṇḍvāvikam*.

[1]The word etc. refers to some blanket (*kambala*).

रजसः क्वचिदुद्रेकस्तमसः क्वचिदिष्यते ।
सत्त्वस्यापि तथोत्कर्षः कुतश्चिदुपजायते ॥१६३॥

In some cases, there is accepted (i.e. noticed) excellence of *rajas* and in some (others) of *tamas*; so also, there is excellence of *sattva* for some reason or other. [163]

That is to say (using the Sāṃkhya terminology): Owing to the variety in the known three *guṇa*s, there are different tainted characters of impressions.

क्वचिदेकप्रधानत्वं कस्मिंश्चिद्द्विषये द्वयोः ।
त्रयाणामपि चान्यत्र ज्ञानकर्मादिचित्रतः ॥१६४॥

In some (case), there is prominence of (any) one (of the *guṇa*s); in some, of two and elsewhere of all the three—this owing to the variety (of an individual's) knowledge and/or activity etc.[1] [164]

This is for justifying the statement in the preceding verse.
[1]The word etc. refers to feeling like attachment.

अग्नेरर्चिर्यथा भाष्वत्सत्त्वोत्कर्षात्तथा मनः ।
पुण्डरीकं यथा शुक्लं सौम्यमाह्लादकृत्तथा ॥१६५॥

As the flame of fire is bright, so is *manas* (bright) owing to the excellence of *sattva* and it is like a lotus, white, gentle and a cause of delight. [165]

This explains *yathāgnyarciḥ*.

सकृद्विद्युद्यथात्यन्तं घनध्वान्तापनोदकृत् ।
अतीव भास्वरास्माकं चक्षुर्मुट्सकृदुज्ज्ञता ॥१६६॥

Just as a single flash of lightning is destroyer of pitch darkness in its fullness, so is (knowledge) extremely bright and has arisen (just) once for blinding the eye. [166]

This explains *yathā sakṛd vidyut* ....

हिरण्यगर्भतत्त्वस्य जायमानस्य केशवात् ।
विद्युद्वत्प्रथते रूपं किल तस्य महात्मनः ॥१६७॥

Then there appears, like lightning, that form of the truth about

Hiraṇyagarbha which is being produced (lit. born) from the great soul Keśava. [167]

Here Sureśvara seems to be under influence of the Vaiṣṇava sect of his times. Cf. verse 122 above. This is stated with a view to praising the Sūtrātman who comes into being after one's death and is characterized by one's last *vāsanā* (desire, or impression).

अतोऽनेनैव रूपेण य उपास्ते दिवानिशम् ।
सर्वान्धकारहन्त्रीव विद्युत्तं श्रीः सदाश्रयेत् ॥१६८॥

Therefore, in him, who meditates day and night on that (Keśava giving rise to Hiraṇyagarbha) in that form, there comes like lightning which destroys all darkness that knowledge, viz. the excellence for him. [168]

नादिर्न मध्यं नैवान्तो नेयत्ता विद्यते यतः ।
अनन्तकल्पोपचयाद्वासनानामुदाहृतिः ॥१६९॥
माहारजनमित्यादिर्न त्वियत्ता विवक्षिता ।
प्रकारदर्शनायैव तेनोदाहृतिरिष्यते ॥१७०॥

Since (in the case of impressions) there is no beginning, no middle, no end and no measure, therefore they are stated (as) example (of the infinite) on account of their increase in mass through numberless *kalpas*. [169]
And in the words *māhārajana* ..., there is not intended any measure (lit. this much of size), therefore, there is stated the example which is indicative of the kind (of numerousness). [170]

A reference to measure is evoked by the six illustrations in BU 2.1.6. Sureśvara intends that one should infer the extent of *vāsanā*s (only) from those six impressions.

Now follows the explanation of the instruction neti neti.

निःशेषमेवं सत्यस्य रूपं व्याख्याय सांप्रतम् ।
परमार्थसत्ययाथात्म्यनिर्देशाय प्रयत्यते ॥१७१॥

Having thus explained completely the form of the truth,[1] now attempt is made to point out the true nature of the highest truth. [171]

[1]That is, from the beginning of Śiśu Brāhmaṇa, viz. *yo ha vai śiśum*, up to *satyasya* which is explained up to verse 170 (on 2.3.6).

यतो व्याख्यातमखिलं मूर्तामूर्तादिवस्त्वतः ।
आदेशोऽनन्तरं तस्य क्रियतेऽनन्यमानिनः ॥१७२॥

Since all the things that begin with *mūrtāmūrta* have been explained, therefore now instruction is given about that person who does not consider himself other than that, viz. Brahman.[1] [172]

This is to explain the purport of *athātaḥ* ...; which is to explain *yo ha vai* ... ending in nominative case. That refers to all the *mūrtāmūrta* things.

[1]The editor of NKL edition paraphrases *ananyamāninaḥ* as *ādeśānyamānarahitasya*.

मूर्तामूर्तस्वभावस्य सत्यस्याविष्कृतेरथ ।
ब्रह्मातिरेकतो नान्यद्यतो वस्त्ववशिष्यते ॥१७३॥
आदेशो ब्रह्मणोऽतोऽयं निरादेशस्य भण्यते ।
अतिमानाभिधानस्य प्रत्यङ्मात्राद्वयात्मनः ॥१७४॥

Now then after[1] the explanation of the truth, which is of the nature of what has a form and what does not have a form, there is nothing else than the Brahman that remains (to be referred to). [173]

Therefore, this is an instruction regarding the Brahman which cannot (really) be instructed about, about which any mention is beyond the means of knowing and which is merely what exists within a human body and (also) the non-dual Ātman. [174]

NKL points out why there is no other *vastu* explained after *mūrta* etc. are explained. SP brings out the purpose of the discussion of the Brahman after that on *satyasya satya*.
[1]This is the purpose of the ablative form *āviṣkṛteḥ*.

कर्मण्यादेशशब्दोऽयं यदि वा करणे भवेत् ।
आदिष्टिरथवादेशो नेति नेत्यद्वयात्मनः ॥१७५॥

This word *ādeśa* signifies an action or the means of action or the very instruction; therefore, (this) instruction *neti neti* has reference to the non-dual Ātman. [175]

This explains the meaning of the word *ādeśa*. Cf. SP (NKL follows it): *ādiśyate iti vyutpattyā brahma*; *ādiśyate 'neneti vyutpattyā śabdo* (*vā*) and *ādiṣṭir iti vyutpattyā jñānam* (*vā ādeśaḥ*).

नेति नेतीतिशब्दाभ्यां सत्यस्य ब्रह्मणः कथम् ।
प्रमाणगोचरातीतं तत्त्वं स्यान्निर्दिदिक्षितम् ॥१७६॥

(A question is asked:) How can there be a reference to the truth, (viz.) the Brahman by the word *neti neti*, if the truth which is beyond what are objects of knowledge? How is it intended to be instructed about? [176]

शृणु सर्वं तदज्ञानसमुत्थस्य निषेधतः ।
प्रत्यङ्मात्रैकरूपेण तदबोधनिराकृतेः ॥१७७॥

Listen. (That is intended to be instructed about), viz. all that which, owing to the denial (or rejection) of what has arisen from ignorance, exists in the form only of the inner self by (its) dispelling ignorance about it(self). [177]

This is in brief the answer to the question above.

अमूर्तस्य परा निष्ठा कारणात्मा पुरोदितः ।
मूर्तस्य च तथा पृथ्वी मध्ये संकीर्णता तयोः ॥१७८॥

The last limit of all that has not a form is earlier said to be the Ātman, as the cause [1] and, in a similar way, the earth (is mentioned) as last limit of what has a form; and between the two there is all variety. [178]

[1]It is the first *vyākṛta* form of the Brahman.

मानाभिधानयोर्यावान्कश्चिद्विषय इष्यते ।
उक्तयोर्मध्यवर्त्येव कार्यकारणयोरसौ ॥१७९॥

Whatever object is accepted as the objects of the means of knowledge and of (having) name is midway between the two, viz. the cause and the effect. [179]

नामरूपे तथा कर्म प्राणा लोकादयस्तथा ।
कारकं वा क्रियान्यद्वा कारणं कार्यमेव च ॥१८०॥
जातिर्गुणः क्रिया द्रव्यं संबन्धो भाव एव च ।
सदसत्सदसच्चेति समस्तव्यस्तमेव च ॥१८१॥
प्रमाता च प्रमाणं च प्रमेयोऽथ क्रियाफले ।
इत्यादेः प्रतिषेधेन प्रत्यङ्मात्रावलम्बिना ॥१८२॥

Name and form, so also action and similarity, *prāṇa*s and regions etc., the means of activity or anything else which is cause and/or effect, [180]
(what is) genus, (what) property, (what) substance and (what) relation and (what) becoming (and) whatever is called existent, non-existent and existent and non-existent, (all that is) collection of things and severality (of things), [181]
the knower and the means of knowing, also the object(s) of knowing, the activity and the result—(all these) by the negation (or denial) of them, depending on merely the inner self (are

but the Brahman). [182]

These verses point to non-existence of anything other than the three mentioned above, viz. the prime cause (i.e. the *avyākṛta* Brahman), the last effect (viz. *pṛthivī*) and whatever is midway between them (viz. water etc.)—this is according to the theory of Bhartṛprapañca.

उपप्रदर्शकोऽशेषनामादेरितिरिष्यते ।
तस्योपदर्शितस्याथ निषेधः क्रियते नञा ॥१८३॥

iti is accepted as indicative of all that has begun with name and now there is indicated the denial of what is shown (above) by the particle *na* (i.e. *nañ*). [183]

This is to signify the purpose served by *na* (in *neti neti*).

आकृष्टं रूपिणो रूपं न पृथग्व्यवतिष्ठते ।
जगत्यकल्पितमपि किमु मोहादिकल्पितम् ॥१८४॥

That form of what has a form, which can be included among the above, does not stand apart in this world, even if it is not conceived; what to say then if it is imagined owing to delusion etc.? [184]

This sets aside a possible view that *kāma* etc. could belong to something else than Brahman, for it is asserted that it does not belong to the Brahman.

घटे पटो निषिद्धोऽपि घटादन्यत्र तिष्ठति ।
तदन्यत्रापि सद्भावादनिषिद्धस्य धर्मिणः ॥१८५॥

(An argument could be made:) A piece of garment, though denied as existent in a pitcher, exists elsewhere than in a pitcher; therefore, whatever has properties can have existence elsewhere than in the existent (viz. Brahman), even if it is denied. [185]

This serves as an illustration for the view that is rejected above.

परमार्थान्निषिद्धस्य तन्मोहोत्थस्य वस्तुनः ।
हिरुक्स्थितिः कथं तस्य परमार्थात्मनाथवा ॥१८६॥

(The answer to this is:) How can there be the existence of a thing elsewhere than in the highest reality, if it has arisen from ignorance about that and is denied, or it is held to be having the nature of the highest Ātman? [186]

Read SP: *ātmano niṣiddhasyānātmano 'nyatra bhedenābhedena vā na sthitī rajatādivat kalpitatvād ity arthaḥ*

निषेध्यानामशेषाणामन्योन्यव्यभिचारतः ।
प्रतीचोऽव्यभिचारोऽतस्तत्राध्यस्तं निषिध्यते ॥१८७॥

Since all the objects that are denied are invariably related mutually and there is non-failing existence of the inner self; therefore, whatever is superimposed on it is denied. [187]

This establishes the *kalpitatva* as leading to unreality.

इतिशब्दोपदिष्टानां निषेधोऽनुभवात्मनि ।
अनन्तेऽन्तवतां यत्र तद्ब्रह्मेत्यवसीयताम् ॥१८८॥

The negation of those, which are indicated by the word *iti*, is in relation to numberless objects that (in reality) exist in the endless Ātman which is the experiencer. Let that be known as the Brahman. [188]

The argument, viz. one could understand the denial of all the objects mentioned before; but thereby is not established the Brahman, is thus answered here.

सद्भावश्चोपलब्धिश्च स्वार्थप्रत्यक्चिदाश्रयात् ।

मूर्तादीनामनिर्देश्यादितिर्मत्तो निवर्तते ॥१८९॥

The existence of the existent, the experience also (of the same) is owing to the sentience, which is within; and that is thanks to the absence of what could be pointed out as having a form etc.; (this is) thus away from 'myself'.[1] [189]

[1]Note in NKL on the word *mattaḥ* 'from me' refers the word to Sureśvara himself but it should be taken to refer to one's *pratyaya* 'awareness' 'I am'.

निषेधति निषेध्यार्थं यद्बलान्नञ्चिदात्मनः ।
विज्ञानेनैव हत्वान्यत्पूर्णत्वेनैति चित्स्वतः ॥१९०॥

That sentient Ātman through whose power the negative particle *na* (technically *nañ*) denies all that is to be denied, after having destroyed all other things by the knowledge through intellect[1] attains its fullness, on its own. [190]

[1]*vijñāna* is here understood as the commonly acquired knowledge.

प्रत्यङ्मात्रदृशि ह्यस्मिञ्जाग्रत्स्वप्नसुषुप्तिषु ।
तदन्यद्यत्तदाभासं तन्नञा प्रतिषिध्यते ॥१९१॥

It is only in this seer, which is but the inner self, that, in the states of waking, dream and sleep, everything else just appears to exist; (all) that is denied by the negative particle *na* (technically *nañ*). [191]

Here is the concluding remark about the denial of all duality.

अविचारितसंसिद्धिप्रत्यङ्मोहहतौ सदा ।
विस्फारिताक्षः प्रत्यग्धीर्मानान्निर्वात्यथात्मनि ॥१९२॥

Ever, when there is destruction of ignorance about the inner self which comes about[1] (even) without thought, there merges in the Ātman,[2] the inner self, possessed of knowledge, with the eyes with (or, fully) open. [192]

[1]That is, gets established.
[2]That is, in its own glory.

अपेक्षाज्ञानहेतूत्थं कार्यकारणवस्त्वतः ।
विचार्यमाणं तन्नास्ति व्योम्नि कार्ष्ण्यमिवात्मनि ॥१९३॥

Therefore, the thing that is related as cause and effect and has arisen from the knowledge of what is expected (as objects),[1] does not, it becomes clear on thought, exist in the Ātman, like darkness in the sky.[2] [193]

[1]That is, depending on outside objects.
[2]It means: as darkness is seen to belong to the sky, even if it really does not.

शब्दप्रवृत्तिहेतूनां प्रत्यगात्मन्यसंभवात् ।
प्रमाणगोचराणां च स्वतः सिद्धेर्न निह्नुतिः ॥१९४॥

Words, activities and causes cannot properly exist in the inner self and are (we notice) as objects of the means of knowledge; they do not get established by themselves. (Therefore,) there is the negation[1] of them. [194]

This explains the raison d'être of the negative particle in the instruction *neti neti*.
[1]It literally means: concealment.

मानाभिधानविषयो यावन्नात्मानमात्मनि ।
लभते प्रत्यगात्मानं न नञ्तावन्निवर्तते ॥१९५॥

So long as the object of knowledge (by means of knowing) and the name does not find itself as existing in the Ātman and (does not become) the inner self, the *na* (*nañ*) (i.e. the particle of denial) does not discontinue. [195]

There is a difference of reading of this verse in NKL and AnSS editions. We follow the latter, though the v.l. in the latter agrees with NKL; cf. *ātmani* in the next verse.

निरस्ताज्ञानतत्कार्ये लब्ध आत्मन्यथात्मना ।
निषेध्यहेतौ प्रध्वस्ते निषेधोऽपि निवर्तते ॥१९६॥

And that negation also ceases to exist when the cause of what is to be denied is destroyed in the inner self by itself when the entire ignorance and its effects are destroyed. [196]

प्रमातृत्वादिना यावत्किंचिदत्र विवक्षितम् ।
तदभावश्च तत्सर्वं नेतीति प्रतिषिध्यते ॥१९७॥

Whatever is here intended to be expressed by the words expressive of the character of an agent etc.[1] and (also is intended) the absence of the same—all that is negated (denied) by the word *neti*. [197]

[1]Cf. specifically verse 182 above but reference to verses 180-181 above is useful.

निषेध्यं सर्वमेवैतदनिषेध्यात्मवस्तुगम् ।
अतो नाभावनिष्ठः स्यादभावस्यापि निह्नवात् ॥१९८॥

All this which is to be negated (finally) culminates into the thing called the Ātman which cannot be negated; therefore, (the negation in *neti neti*) does not end into the absence of anything, because there is the negation of even the absence (of every object negated). [198]

This explains the purport of the repetition of *neti* and how there is not *anavasthā* resulting from the negation of the negator.

नेति नेतीत्यतो वीप्सा जिघृक्षितनिषेधतः ।
बुभुत्सितस्य कृत्स्नस्य वीप्सैवातो निषेधनी ॥१९९॥

Therefore, this repetition in *neti neti* proceeds to negate whatever is sought to be taken up (or, postulated by any objector) and, therefore, this repetition is the negator of all that is *sought* to be known.[1] [199]

[1]This means: an object conceived as what is to be known.

ज्ञानक्रियाभ्यां व्याप्योऽयमित्याकाङ्क्षा निवर्तते ।
अप्रमित्सित एकस्मिन्निष्ठां यात्यचिकीर्षिते ॥२००॥

The expectancy of (some thing as) what is to be pervaded (i.e. grasped) by knowledge and activity (then) ceases to be. And the final end (of the intellect)[1] is achieved with respect to that alone which is not sought to be known and/or which is not sought to be effected. [200]

[1]Namely, the knowledge of the uniqueness or singleness (*aikya*) of the Ātman.

रज्जुयाथात्म्यविज्ञानात्सर्पवत्कारणात्मनः ।
निषेधो नान्यतः शक्यः कर्तुं वर्षशतैरपि ॥२०१॥

It is not possible, even for hundred years, to effect the negation of anything other than the Ātman which is (held as) the cause (of all existence) in the same way as there cannot be negation (of a serpent on knowing) the true nature of a rope [which is the cause (of the false apprehension)]. [201]

यद्यत्प्राप्तं जगत्यस्मिंस्तत्तत्सर्वं निषिध्यते ।
एवं च सत्यनिर्दिष्टाशङ्कापि विनिवर्तते ॥२०२॥

Whatever is obtained here in this world is all of it negated; (and) thus even a doubt (that can be) expressed regarding the truth ceases to exist (i.e. disappears). [202]

This expresses the effect of the instruction *neti neti*.

न चेद्वीप्सा तदा वाक्यद्वयमेतद्विवक्षितम् ।
उक्तद्वयनिषेधेन तस्य चोपक्षयाद्भवेत् ॥२०३॥
अनुक्तविषयाशङ्का सर्वस्याप्रतिषेधतः ।
यदि वाभावविषया न ह्यभावो निषिध्यते ॥२०४॥

If there were no repetition (of the word *neti*), then there could be those two sentences intended by an objector: (i) by the negation of the pair that is already stated (*mūrtāmūrta*) and there could arise after the cessation of that (pair) [203] a doubt about some object that has not been stated there would not be the negation of all; (ii) or, perhaps, this would refer to only the absence of some object(s); and, indeed, an absence is not negated. [204]

साक्षान्मानप्रसिद्धेषु प्रतिषिद्धेतरग्रहः ।
अप्रसिद्धे प्रसिद्धानां निषेधाच्छून्यताग्रहः ॥२०५॥

(In the objects), that are established by the direct means of knowing, there can be acceptance of things other than those negated and there could be understanding of nothingness from the negation of the known things, with respect to unknown objects (if any). [205]

Sureśvara implies that the negation *neti neti* does not refer to avoid the result of negation (viz. the knowledge of the Brahman), because the Brahman is already known in the form of 'I am'.

आदेश इत्युपक्रम्य प्रतिषेधोऽयमुच्यते ।
साक्षादादिश्यते येन तादृगादेश उच्यते ॥२०६॥

Beginning with the word '(this is) instruction' there is stated the negation and thus there is a direct instruction (about the Brahman), since such is the instruction of the Brahman. [206]

Read SP (NKL agreeing with it in substance): *brahmaṇa ādeśa ity uktvā niṣedhokter ayam ādeśo niṣedhākhya brahmaprati-*

pādanapara evety arthaḥ.

निषेधवर्त्मना तस्मादनिषेध्यात्मसाक्षिणा ।
ज्ञाताज्ञातं निषिध्याथ सदा दृष्टौ प्रतिष्ठति ॥२०७॥

Therefore, having negated by this way of negation, (all that) which has the Ātman as its seer, that cannot be negated, viz. all known and unknown (things), one settles down in the state of a knower (lit. a seer).[1] [207]

[1]It literally means: in the state of knowing.

यथा श्रोत्रधिया रूपं रूपहेत्वसमन्वयात् ।
नाग्रहीन्न च गृह्णाति न ग्रहीष्यति शब्दवत् ॥२०८॥
प्रत्यक्तत्त्वे विनिर्ज्ञाते नेति नेतीतिवाक्यतः ।
तद्वत्सकारणोऽनात्मा नाभूदस्ति भविष्यति ॥२०९॥

As, by the knowledge through the sense of hearing, one has (never) grasped, nor does one grasp and will grasp, like a form, (even as one grasps) a wind since (one's action is not related to the cause of form); [208]
in the same way, when truth of the inner self becomes known from the sentence *neti neti*, there has not been, is not and will not be any non-Ātman together with its cause (viz. the ignorance about the nature of the Ātman). [209]

नान्यदज्ञानतोऽस्तित्वं द्वितीयस्यात्मनो यथा ।
निवृत्तिस्तद्वदेवास्य नावगत्यात्मनोऽपरा ॥२१०॥

As there is no existence of what is other than the Ātman except from the ignorance (about the nature of it), similarly there will be cessation of this (ignorance) which cannot consist in anything else than in the knowledge of the Ātman. [210]

अनन्यायत्तमैकात्म्यं यदा साक्षाद्व्यवस्थितम् ।
ब्येव त्वेति प्रतिज्ञेयं तदा स्यात्सफलोदिता ॥२११॥

When this uniqueness (or singleness) of the Ātman, which has been thus directly obtained, as it does not depend on another, then, therefore, this enunciation, viz. *vy eva tvā*, would be described (i.e. considered) as fruitful. [211]

नेति नेतीत्यतो वीप्सासंभवादुक्तवस्तुनः ।
कृतार्थता तथा च स्यादन्यथा नोपपद्यते ॥२१२॥

Therefore, from the repetition in the statement *neti neti*, there results meaningfulness of the thing[1] that is stated and of that anything otherwise does not reasonably exist. [212]

[1]Of *aikātmyajñāna*, or better perhaps, of the enunciation *vy eva tvā*.

परागर्थेषु सक्ता धीः प्रत्यगर्थानुरञ्जनात् ।
निषिद्धातः परागर्थात्प्रतीचि लभते स्थितिम् ॥२१३॥

(Therefore) one's intellect, which is fixed on objects outside, is warded off from the objects outside and then, being tainted by the thing within (viz. the inner self), becomes steady in that thing within. [213]

So far, Sureśvara explains the meaning of the sentence neti neti ... ādeśaḥ in agreement with BUB. Now, he explains it as an informative injunction regarding the inner self.

व्यतिरेकस्य सिद्धत्वादादेशोक्तेः पुरैव हि ।
साक्षाद्ब्रह्मत्वसिद्ध्यर्थमादेशोऽयमथोच्यते ॥२१४॥

Now, this instruction (viz. *neti neti*) is stated here for establishing that the Brahman is patent to oneself, since the meaning of instruction which has been already established through (conveying) the distinction of the Brahman from (the *mūrtāmūrta* things) is already known. [214]

This is the explanation of the instruction *neti neti* given by

Sureśvara.

This argument presupposes the distinction between the Brahman and the *mūrtāmūrta* things by the very use of the genitive in the expression *brahmaṇaḥ* (*dve rūpe*). The words *neti neti* only confirm the distinction.

न निषेधो निषेध्यार्थो लक्षणार्थपरत्वतः ।
ब्रह्मणो मान्तरासिद्धेः शून्यतैव प्रसज्यते ॥२१५॥

The negation (in *neti neti*) does not pertain to what is to be negated, since it is the purport of indicating (the Brahman). Since the Brahman is not established by any other means,[1] therefore there could have followed only void.[2] [215]

This is to explain why the negation in the instruction *neti neti* does not purport only to negate the *mūrta* etc.

[1]This refers to anything else than the statement in the Upaniṣad about the Brahman (*brahmaparavākya*).

[2]This reaffirms that the negation does not pertain only to what is to be negated, which implies that nothing else than that existed.

षष्ठ्युक्तेरेव संसिद्धा मूर्तादेर्ब्रह्मणोऽन्यता ।
ततश्च जामितासक्तिर्नातः स्यात्पारिशेष्यगीः ॥२१६॥

By (lit. from the statement with the use of genitive in *brahmaṇaḥ dve* ...) it gets established that the *mūrta* etc. are different from the Brahman and from that there necessarily (or contingently) follows the relation (of what is negated to the Brahman); therefore from this (sentence *neti neti*) (one is) not (to understand) a statement of the remainder.[1] [216]

[1]Namely, of what remains after the *mūrta* and *amūrta* are stated.

शक्यते न निषेद्धुं च प्रत्यक्षाद्याश्रितत्वतः ।
निषेधान्न पुमर्थोऽपि कश्चित्सिध्येत्समीहितः ॥२१७॥

It is not possible to negate (the mass of *mūrtāmūrta*), since it is dependent on direct perception etc.[1] and also the end of human beings (viz. *mokṣa* or *brahmajñāna*) which is desired (by men) will not result from mere negation. [217]

This is to affirm that the sentence *neti neti* does not purport merely to negate *mūrtāmūrta*; but it conveys the knowledge of the Brahman.

[1]This refers to other means of knowing.

निषेधमात्रनिष्ठत्वे न चादेशो भवेत्प्रभोः ।
ब्रह्म मूर्तादि नेत्युक्तौ मूर्तादेर्न निषेधगीः ॥२१८॥

Being merely for negation (of *mūrta* etc.), there would not be the instruction about the lord[1] and by a statement, viz. 'Brahman is not *mūrta*' etc., there cannot be negation of *mūrta* etc. [218]

This is to say: The instruction *neti neti* cannot be merely for rejection of others; nor can the denial of the Brahman to be *mūrta* etc. give rise to the knowledge of it.

[1]That is, the all-pervading Brahman.

ततश्च ब्रह्मतासिद्धिर्द्वितीये सति वस्तुनि ।
व्येव त्वेति प्रतिज्ञार्थो नापि चाविष्कृतो भवेत् ॥२१९॥
पारिशेष्यादतोऽसिद्धिः स्याद्विवक्षितवस्तुनः ।
यथा सिद्धिस्तथा व्याख्या कार्येहोक्तेरतोऽञ्जसा ॥२२०॥

And from that there would not be the establishing of the Brahman if it were taken as a thing other (than the negated) and also the purport of the enunciation *vy eva tvā* would not become revealed. [219]

Therefore, there is no establishing of the thing which is intended to be expressed by the rule of the remainder.[1] Therefore, the explanation of the statement (*neti neti*) should be offered in such a way that there would be established (that thing only) smoothly. [220]

In verses 219-220ab there is a refutation of two views regarding the meaning of *neti*: (a) negation of all knowables, (b) establishing Brahman as what remains. And verse 220cd states the purport of *neti neti* as a suitable expression of the existence of the Brahman.

[1]That is, the Brahman is what remains after the *mūrta* etc. are already described.

सिद्धो निषेधः प्रागेव सर्वस्यानात्मवस्तुनः ।
प्रत्यग्याथात्म्यविज्ञानादन्योन्यव्यभिचारतः ॥२२१॥

Negation of all non-Ātman things has been already[1] established by the knowledge of the true nature of the inner self and on account of the mutual exclusion of the non-Ātman things. [221]

[1]Refer to verse 216 above.

अन्योन्यव्यभिचारोऽस्य वीक्ष्यतेऽनात्मवस्तुनः ।
स्वरूपव्यभिचारोऽपि सुषुप्तादौ स्वसाक्षिगः ॥२२२॥
यथा मात्रादिसत्तेयं प्रत्यक्संवित्तिसिद्धिका ।
प्रमात्रादेरभावोऽपि प्रत्यग्बोधाश्रयात्तथा ॥२२३॥
अविचारितसंसिद्धिरात्माविद्यैकरूपतः ।
सिद्धायतेऽखिलोऽनात्मा स्वतःसिद्धात्मसंश्रयात् ॥२२४॥
अतिरोहितसंवित्को व्यपास्ताशेषविक्रियः ।
अनन्यमातृमानादिर्दृष्टिमात्रात्मकत्वतः ॥२२५॥

This mutual exclusion of the non-Ātmans is (already) seen and also the exclusion of their own forms is noticed in the state of sleep etc.; and which is perceived by the inner self. [222]

As this existence of the means of knowing etc.[1] is established by the knowledge of the self within, so also the absence of

the knower etc.[2] is similarly established by resorting to the knowledge of the inner self. [223]
The entire (mass of) non-Ātman appears to get established owing to its being of the nature only of ignorance about (the nature of) the Ātman and is thus established without (even a) thought and on account of its dependence on the self-established Ātman, [224]
(Who is thus self-established) because sentience in it does not remain concealed, because it has discarded the entire mass of modifications and because it is of the nature of only the seer (lit. seeing) and has no other knower or means of knowing. [225]

[1]The word etc. refers to *meya* and *māna* [beside *mātṛ* (possibly) the means of knowing].
[2]The word etc. refers to *prameya* and *pramāṇa* (i.e. the act of knowing and/or the means of knowing).

भावाभावात्मिका सिद्धिर्येयं सर्वाप्यनात्मनः ।
तद्विरुद्धात्मकान्मत्तो मय्येवासौ प्रसिध्यति ॥२२६॥

Whatever be (pointed out) as the establishing of the presence and the absence of the entire non-Ātman, it is established owing to the awareness of only 'from me' and 'in me'.[1] [226]

[1]From the Ātman which is known as I (*aham*) and from me (*mattaḥ*). Cf. verse 189 above and note thereon regarding *mattaḥ*.
Sureśvara often uses pronominal forms like *aham*, *mayi* and *tava* and lends to his writing the form of some direct conversation. There is nevertheless the purport of conveying an individual self.

अनन्यानुभवेनैव भावाभावात्मभूमिषु ।
प्रत्यक्कूटस्थ आत्मानं पश्यन्नास्ते फलात्मना ॥२२७॥

Through the experience of none else does the inner self, the immutable one, see itself in the various levels of the presence and the absence (of things), and thus sees itself as of the nature of the fruit (viz. right knowledge). [227]

This sets aside the notion of an inner self needing the help of another and so on in infinite regress.

AnSS suggests *-sthaṃ* as a v.l. reading, but both commentaries do not show and support this.

अतो मात्रादिसंभेदो यत्र यत्र निवर्तते ।
तत्र तत्रैकलः प्रत्यक्स्वमहिम्नैव सिध्यति ॥२२८॥

Therefore, whatever these distinctions of organs (or means) etc. cease to exist, there does the single inner self remain owing to its own glory [1] (or power) alone. [228]

Refer to verse 223 above.

[1]Cf. verse 192 above. Also refer to *yadbalāt* in verse 190 above.

प्रमात्रादेरभावोऽतो यः सिद्धः स्वात्मबोधतः ।
नञ्वृत्तिस्तं सदाबुद्धं लक्षयत्यपृथक्प्रमम् ॥२२९॥

Therefore, the absence of the agent (of knowing) etc. is established as (or, is caused by) the knowledge of the Ātman. The function of the negation-particle (*nañ*) indicates [1] the ever awake Ātman which does not have any distinction from knowledge.[2] [229]

Refer to note 2 on verse 223 above.

[1]This means that *nañ* conveys the meaning of the inner self, i.e. it does not express the same; it only indicates it. The reason for this is stated in the next verse.

[2]NKL reads in the end *apṛthakprabham*.

वैविक्त्यान्न च मानादेरनन्यानुभवात्मनि ।
सहेतुकस्य वृत्तिः स्यान्नित्यबोधावबोधिनि ॥२३०॥

Owing to the distinction of the means of knowing etc. which have some cause (for their existence) there cannot be any functioning of them in the case of (the Ātman) which is of the nature of experience of nothing else than itself and which ever enlightens itself. [230]

This explains why the Ātman is indicated (i.e. not expressed) by the particle of negation, viz. *nañ*.

अविद्याद्यतिरेकेण कारणादिविधर्मकं ।
लब्धमात्मात्मकं वस्तु प्रतीचोऽनन्यमानतः ॥२३१॥

This thing which is of the nature of the Ātman is obtained (i.e. known) from the inner self which does not have any other means for (revealing) itself—this thing which is in nature opposed to causes etc. and which is other than ignorance etc.[1] [231]

This is for justifying the word *vaiviktyāt* in the preceding verse.
[1]The word etc. refers to *avidyāphala* its effects.

एतद्वस्तु स्वतःसिद्धं प्रमात्राद्यनपेक्षतः ।
सर्वस्यैव ततः सिद्धेः कथं सिध्येत्तदन्यतः ॥२३२॥

This thing (i.e. Ātman) is self-established, being independent of any knower etc.[1] and, since all (the knowables in the world) get established on its account, how can it (i.e. the Ātman) get established by something else? [232]

[1]Refer to note 2 on verse 223 above.

उक्ता प्रमेयसंसिद्धिः स्वमहिम्नैव नञ्श्रुतेः ।
तस्य ब्रह्मत्वबोधाय नेति ब्रह्मेतिनोच्यते ॥२३३॥

From this hearing of *nañ* is thus the establishing of what is to be known (viz. the Ātman) owing to its own power (or, glory); for the knowledge of that as the Brahman (the word) *iti* in *neti* expresses that. [233]

This is to point out that *nañ* primarily refers to the object (i.e. *tvaṃ padārtha*), because the Brahman is self-established; *iti* refers to the *mūrta* etc.

आत्मप्रत्ययमामेयो लक्षितो यो नञाञ्जसा ।
अविद्यादेस्तदात्मत्वादिति ब्रह्मेति बोध्यते ॥२३४॥

It is conveyed (lit. made known) that the Brahman is that (one) which is smoothly indicated by (the negative particle) *nañ* and which is the knowable (i.e. to be known)[1] by the awareness of (one's own) self owing to ignorance etc.[2] which is its nature. [234]

The argument is Jīva 'the inner conscience' is subjected to worldly dealings and yet it is the Brahman. So it is indicated by *nañ*.

[1]*māmeya* means *meya* 'knowable (or what is to be known)' from *mā* 'knowledge' in the worldly dealings (*pramāṇapra-meya-vyavahāra*).

[2]The word etc. refers to the effect(s) of *avidyā*.

प्रत्यङ्मोहतदुत्थस्य प्रत्यग्याथात्म्यबोधतः ।
बाधितत्वादतोऽवोचदिति ब्रह्मेति मोहनुत् ॥२३५॥

Owing to the rise of the knowledge of the true nature of the inner self from the delusion (about the nature of) the inner self and the product (i.e. ignorance) of it, (the Śruti) states *iti* in order to convey that (the Ātman is) the Brahman, (and it is thus) the remover of delusion. [235]

Now follows the discussion of the meaning of the sentence na hy etasmād iti netyantat paraṃ asti.

आदेशं प्रत्यतिमहानथात इति संभ्रमः ।
तेनासदृश आदेशो नन्वयुक्तोऽयमीर्यते ।२३६॥

(An objection may be raised:) Indeed, this instruction is improperly given, since it is not a proper instruction; for there is very great confusion about (or, misgiving as to the purpose of) the instruction. [236]

युक्त एवायमादेशो न यतो विद्यते परः ।
आदेशोऽतोऽयमेवात्र ब्रह्मण्यादेश इष्यते ॥२३७॥

(The answer is:) Indeed, this instruction is but proper, since there is no other (instruction elsewhere in the Śruti). Therefore, this itself is desired as instruction about the Brahman. [237]

आदिदिक्षितमेतस्य तत्त्वं यद्ब्रह्मणः परम् ।
यावन्तस्तत्र निर्देश्यास्तेऽर्थाः सर्वे निवर्तिताः ॥२३८॥

Since the highest truth about this Brahman is intended to be under instruction, whatever are there the objects to be pointed out (by words etc.) they are all of them set aside (by the words *neti neti*). [238]

This justifies the statement *na yato vidyate paraḥ* in the preceding verse.

निवृत्तिश्च यथोक्तैव तेषामैकात्म्यलक्षणा ।
भिन्नदेशस्थितिस्त्वत्र वास्तवी नोपपद्यते ॥२३९॥

And the cessation (of the duality, viz. *mūrta* etc.) is (effected) just as stated (before), viz. it is of the nature of a single Ātman (in the case) of them.[1] And their actual existence in different places here (i.e. in this world) cannot stand to reason.[2] [239]

[1]This refers to the objects, viz. *mūrta* etc.
[2]Alternatively, cannot be reasonably accepted (as real).

अव्यावृत्ताननुगतो ब्रह्मशब्दार्थ इष्यते ।
मुख्योऽन्यस्मिन्सति यतो ब्रह्मार्थो नावसीयते ॥२४०॥

शब्दप्रवृत्तिहेतूनामैकात्म्येन समाप्तितः ।
तथा तदभिधेयानामादेशोऽयं मतः परः ॥२४१॥

It is accepted that the object signified by the word Brahman is not distinguished from other (objects) and is not similar to any other(s) because this object, viz. the Brahman, is not understood as the principal meaning of the word (*śabda*) (in *brahmaśabda*) (if there existed any other object). [240]
Since it is (thus) understood (lit. obtained) those which have caused the functions of words, viz. those which are signified by them, are only the Ātman, therefore, this instruction is understood as the highest.[1] [241]

[1]That is, the highest conveyer of the truth.

अभिधाभिधेयसंबन्धमङ्गीकृत्य यतोऽक्षरे ।
न कश्चिदपि शब्दोऽत्र साक्षाद्ब्रह्मणि वर्तते ॥२४२॥

(This is so) because not a single word refers to the Brahman itself after accepting the relationship between expression[1] and what is signified by it. [242]

[1]It can stand for word or for the primary function of words.

आदेशो नेति नेत्येव तेनेह घटतेऽञ्जसा ।
तदबोधप्रसूतानामाकाङ्क्षाणां निषेधतः ॥२४३॥

Therefore, the instruction in the words *neti neti* gets, smoothly construed (in respect of the truth to be conveyed by the Śruti), owing to its rejection of all the expectancies which arise from ignorance about it (viz. Brahman). [243]

Now follows the exposition of the meaning of atha nāmadheyaṃ satyasya satyam iti prāṇā vai satyaṃ teṣām eva satyam.

मूर्तामूर्तं हि सत्याह्वं प्राणाः सत्यास्तदात्मतः ।
क्षेत्रज्ञस्तदुपाधित्वात्सत्य इत्यभिधीयते ॥२४४॥

Since (the mass of) *mūrtāmūrta* is called *satya*, *prāṇa*s (organs etc.) are also (called or described as) *satya*, on account of their having that (viz. *satya*) as their nature, and, therefore, the knower of the field is also called *satya*, for it has them as its limiting adjuncts. [244]

अनिर्देश्यस्य निर्देश्या ये भेदाः कार्यलक्षणाः ।
तेषु लब्धास्पदं नाम परस्मिन्नुपचर्यते ॥२४५॥

The noun which has found scope in those distinct objects, having the nature of effects, and which can be signified (by words), of what cannot be signified (by words) is transferred to the highest (reality, i.e. Brahman). [245]

This is to explain why the Brahman also is signified by the word *satya* even after *satyasya* (in genitive) expresses what can be signified in words.

मूर्तामूर्तात्मकं सत्यं प्राणादेः कार्यरूपिणः ।
तस्याप्येतत्परं सत्यं यन्नेतीत्यवधारितम् ॥२४६॥

What is specified in the word *neti* is this highest truth of the *prāṇa*s (viz. the organs) etc. which is of the nature of effects and is (commonly known) as truth and (is known) in the form of *mūrtāmūrta*. [246]

In *satyasya satyam*, the two words occur respectively in genitive and nominative forms. In the earlier verse, the word *satya* (in genitive) has been explained and, now, the word *satya* (in nominative) is explained.

उक्तवस्त्वतिरेकेण नामीषां सत्यता यतः ।
न चाप्यसत्यता तस्मात्तेषां सत्यं परं पदम् ॥२४७॥

Since all these do not have any true nature other than (that of) the said thing (viz. the Ātman), therefore, they do not have (any) untrue nature and their truth is the highest truth (viz. the Brahman). [247]

This is to state that the word *satya* can be applicable (in final reality) to the world also.

आत्मवन्तो यथा रज्ज्वा रज्जुसर्पादयस्तथा ।
आत्मवन्तो निरात्मानः प्राणाद्याः प्रत्यगात्मना ॥२४८॥

As a serpent in a rope etc. come to have existence (*ātmavantaḥ*) through only a rope, similarly, *prāṇa*s etc. which are non-Ātman come to have existence only through the inner self. [248]

The statement in the preceding verse is clarified by citing an example.

यत एवमतोऽन्वीक्ष्य मूर्तामूर्तादिवर्त्मना ।
सत्यशब्दाभिधेयार्थं तया द्वारा परं पदम् ॥२४९॥
व्यपदिश्यमानमैकात्म्यं सत्यस्यात्मानमद्वयम् ।
द्रष्टव्यमात्मनैवैनं सत्यं पश्येद्यथोदितम् ॥२५०॥

Since this is so, (therefore) having understood the meaning of what is signified by the word *satya* by way of understanding the *mūrtāmūrta* etc. and in that way (should one see) the highest truth; [249]
the nature of their being but the unique or single Ātman which is thus conveyed by the word (*satya*),[1] viz. the non-dual Ātman, (that is) to be seen—thus should one see this truth which is thus described. [250]

[1]NKL edition reads *ucyamānam aikātmyam*.

अतोऽव्याकृतयाथात्म्यं व्याकृतेनोपदिश्यते ।
सत्यस्य सत्यमिति तन्नान्यथा व्यपदेशभाक् ॥२५१॥

Therefore in the words *satyasya satyam* is conveyed the nature of the unmodified by means of (the statement about) the modified; that cannot be conveyed by any other words. [251]

This sets aside the possible argument that the word *satya* cannot signify the Brahman, since that use of the word cannot be proved useful in the way of continued *anvaya* of it with the same.

व्यपदेशाय नामैतन्न स्वं नामास्य विद्यते ।
ननु ब्रह्माक्षरमिति व्यपदेशोऽत्र नामभिः ॥२५२॥

All this is for conveying (that) it has no name (i.e. noun) of its own. But[1] indeed this reference, viz. *brahma akṣaram* ..., is but use of names.[2] [252]

[1]This is an objection.
[2]That is, for signifying it.

कार्यकारणगे तत्त्वे नाम लब्धास्पदं यतः ।
रूपाभिधेयसंबन्धागरूपाशब्दमक्षरम् ॥२५३॥
लक्षयेन्नाञ्जसा वक्ति परं ब्रह्म कथंचन ।
शब्दप्रवृत्तिहेतूनां साक्षाद्ब्रह्मण्यसंभवात् ॥२५४॥

Since the name (i.e. noun) has found relevance on the truth which exists in the causes and effects and it has relation to form and names though it (itself) has no form, no word for its description and it is imperishable— [253]
that name indicates it, since it can never express smoothly the highest Brahman in any way. (This is so) because, in the case of the Brahman, there is no direct relationship with the causes of functions of the words. [254]

In these verses Sureśvara answers the objection and gives his idea of *lakṣaṇā* to be understood in such Upaniṣadic sentences as convey the nature of the Brahman.

इति श्रीबृहदारण्यकोपनिषद्भाष्यवार्तिके द्वितीयाध्यायस्य
तृतीयं ब्राह्मणम् ॥३॥

****

SELECT GLOSSARY

(1) Here are given mostly such words [or, almost all of them] in the text under consideration as Sureśvara used in their peculiar senses.
(2) Figures after the specified meanings are the numbers of verse in the text: those from 2.3 are distinguished from those in 2.2 by prefixing 2. to them.

akṣasūtra	the beads and the thread (in a rosary) (33)
abhyāhita	residing in (2.8)
āhvāna	name (=*abhidhāna*) (2.30)
upaniṣad	(=*upāsanā*) (made of) worship (1)
	the secret doctrines (2.6, 2.7)
	the Upaniṣadic statement (2.22, 90)
kaliṅga	Sūtrātman or Hiraṇyagarbha (47)
kṛṣṇasāra	dark pupil of the eye (41)
cakṣus	the orb of the sun (70)
tamasvin	possessed of (20)
nyāya	a Śruti statement (expressive of) reason (52)
	the statement of reason (=guiding principle) (52, 57), cf. the reason for establishing the statement of the Śruti in the popular way of reason (see 53 note)
	reason (52, 112, 129, 138)
pratyāhita	residing especially (2.8, 13, 24); cp. *abhyāhita* above
pratyāhṛtya	by putting together, i.e. having connected them *(=saṃbadhya)* (17)

māhārajana	painted with turmeric (103, 153, 160, 170)
moha	delusion (11, 156, 184, 235); cf. *vyāmoha* (86)
rasa	essence (or, cause) (37, 38, 44, 46-51, 56, 58-61; cf. 63)
liṅga	=Virāj (47); =Hiraṇyagarbha (48);
	subtle (64, 81, 84, 85, 86, 116, 118, 121, 128, 149)
	the subtle form (of a living being) (60, 117, 152, 159, 161, 162)
vikāra	modification (=*lakṣaṇa*, =*upādhi*) (91)
vijñāna	the Sūtra, the subtle form of a living being (20, 53)
	knowledge obtained by intellect (108, 190)
vijñānātman	=*jīvātman*, =*kṣetrajña* (96 etc.)
vyāviddha	what has appeared (=*vyākṛta*) (96)
saṃgati	lit. going together, i.e. association with one another (17)
satattva	(=*svarūpa*) nature (2.5, 3)
sāmānyavṛtti	common function (2.11)
sūtrita	enunciated (in physical sense) (2.3)
sthāna	orb (=*maṇḍala*) (41)

****

BIBLIOGRAPHY

TEXTS

Brahmasūtraśāṅkarabhāṣya with the Commentaries Bhāmatī, Kalpataru and Parimala. Bombay: Nirnayasagar Press, 1917.

Bṛhadāraṇyakopaniṣad with Śaṅkara's Commentary. AnSS 15, Poona: 1891.

Bṛhadāraṇyakopaniṣadbhāṣyavārtika with Ānandagiri's Commentary Śāstraprakāśikā. 3 vols., AnSS 16, Poona: 1892-94.

Bṛhadāraṇyakavārtikasāra of Vidyāraṇya. Chowkhamba Sanskrit Series Nos. 205-208, 243-244, 257-258, 271-272, Benares: 1915-19.

Nyāyakalpalatikā. vol.2, (ed.) V. Subramanya Sastri, Tirupati: Kendriya Sanskrit Vidyapeeth, 1975.

Manusmṛti with Kullūka's Commentary Manvarthamuktāvali. Bombay: Nirnayasagar Press, 1946.

BOOKS

Jog, K. P. and S. Hino, *Advaita Tradition Series.* 12 vols., Delhi: Motilal Banarsidass.

vol. 1 (1982): Hino, *Sureśvara's Vārtika on Yājñavalkya-Maitreyī Dialogue.*

vol. 2 (1988): Jog and Hino, *Sureśvara's Vārtika on Madhu Brāhmaṇa.*

vol. 3 (1990): Hino and Jog, *Sureśvara's Vārtika on Aśva and Aśvamedha Brāhmaṇa.*

vol. 4 (1991): Jog and Hino, *Sureśvara's Vārtika on Udgītha Brāhmaṇa.*

vol. 5 (1993): Jog and Hino, *Sureśvara's Vārtika on Puruṣavidha Brāhmaṇa.*

vol. 6 (1995): Hino and Jog, *Sureśvara's Vārtika on Saptānna Brāhmaṇa.*

Mahadevan, T.M.P. (ed. and tr.) *The Saṃbandha-Vārtika of Sureśvarācārya*. Madras: University of Madras, 1972.

Limaye, V.P. and R.D. Vadekar, *Eighteen Principal Upaniṣads*. vol.1, Poona: Vaidika Samshodana Mandala, 1958.

Madhavananda, S., (tr.) *The Bṛhadāraṇyaka Upaniṣad*. Calcutta: Advaita Ashrama, 1975.

Röer, E., (tr.) *The Twelve Principal Upaniṣads*. vol.2, Madras: Theosophical Publishing House, 1931.

****

HALF-VERSE INDEX

****